Casenotes Legal Briefs

COPYRIGHT

Adaptable to courses utilizing Goldstein's casebook on Copyright, Patent, Trademark and Related State Doctrines

NORMAN S. GOLDENBERG, SENIOR EDITOR
PETER TENEN, MANAGING EDITOR

STAFF WRITERS

KEMP RICHARDSON
PATRICIA P. LAIACONA

PUBLISHED BY **CASENOTES PUBLISHING CO., INC. 1640 5th ST., SUITE 208 SANTA MONICA, CA 90401**

ISBN 0-87457-173-1

FORMAT OF THE CASENOTE LEGAL BRIEF

CASE CAPSULE: This bold-faced section (first three paragraphs) highlights the procedural nature of the case, a short summary of the facts, and the rule of law. This is an invaluable quick-review device designed to refresh the student's memory for classroom discussion and exam preparation.

NATURE OF CASE: This section identifies the form of action (e.g., breach of contract, negligence, battery), the type of proceeding (e.g., demurrer, appeal from trial court's jury instructions) and the relief sought (e.g., damages, injunction, criminal sanctions).

FACT SUMMARY: The fact summary is included to refresh the student's memory. It can be used as a quick reminder of the facts when the student is chosen by an instructor to brief a case.

CONCISE RULE OF LAW: This portion of the brief summarizes the general principle of law that the case illustrates. Like the fact summary, it is included to refresh the student's memory. It may be used for instant recall of the court's holding and for classroom discussion or home review.

FACTS: This section contains all relevant facts of the case, including the contentions of the parties and the lower court holdings. It is written in a logical order to give the student a clear understanding of the case. The plaintiff and defendant are identified by their proper names throughout and are always labeled with a (P) or (D).

ISSUE: The issue is a concise question that brings out the essence of the opinion as it relates to the section of the casebook in which the case appears. Both substantive and procedural issues are included if relevant to the decision.

HOLDING AND DECISION: This section offers a clear and in-depth discussion of the rule of the case and the court's rationale. It is written in easy-to-understand language. When relevant, it includes a thorough discussion of the exceptions listed by the court, the concurring and dissenting opinions, and the names of the judges.

CONCURRENCE / DISSENT: All concurrences and dissents are briefed whenever they are included by the casebook editor.

EDITOR'S ANALYSIS: This last paragraph gives the student a broad understanding of where the case "fits in" with other cases in the section of the book and with the entire course. It is a hornbook-style discussion indicating whether the case is a majority or minority opinion and comparing the principal case with other cases in the casebook. It may also provide analysis from restatements, uniform codes, and law review articles. The editor's analysis will prove to be invaluable to classroom discussion.

CROSS-REFERENCE TO OUTLINE: Wherever possible, following each case is a cross-reference linking the subject matter of the issue to the appropriate place in the *Casenote Law Outline,* which provides further information on the subject.

WINTER v. G.P. PUTNAM'S SONS

938 F.2d 1033 (1991).

NATURE OF CASE: Appeal from summary judgment in a products liability action.

FACT SUMMARY: Winter (P) relied on a book on mushrooms published by Putnam (D) and became critically ill after eating a poisonous mushroom.

CONCISE RULE OF LAW: Strict products liability is not applicable to the expressions contained within a book.

FACTS: Winter (P) purchased The Encyclopedia of Mushrooms, a book published by Putnam (D), to help in collecting and eating wild mushrooms. In 1988, Winter (P), relying on descriptions in the book, ate some wild mushrooms which turned out to be poisonous. Winter (P) became so ill he required a liver transplant. He brought a strict products liability action against Putnam (D), alleging that the book contained erroneous and misleading information that caused his injury. Putnam (D) responded that the information in the book was not a product for purposes of strict products liability, and the trial court granted its motion for summary judgment. The trial court also rejected Winter's (P) actions for negligence and misrepresentation. Winter (P) appealed.

ISSUE: Is strict products liability applicable to the expressions contained within a book?

HOLDING AND DECISION: (Sneed, J.) No. Strict products liability is not applicable to the expressions contained within a book. Products liability is geared toward tangible objects. The expression of ideas is governed by copyright, libel, and misrepresentation laws. The Restatement (Second) of Torts lists examples of the items that are covered by §402A strict liability. All are tangible items, such as tires or automobiles. There is no indication that the doctrine should be expanded beyond this area. Furthermore, there is a strong public interest in the unfettered exchange of ideas. The threat of liability without fault could seriously inhibit persons who wish to share thoughts and ideas with others. Although some courts have held that aeronautical charts are products for purposes of strict liability, these charts are highly technical tools which resemble compasses. The Encyclopedia of Mushrooms, published by Putnam (D), is a book of pure thought and expression and therefore does not constitute a product for purposes of strict liability. Additionally, publishers do not owe a duty to investigate the contents of books that they distribute. Therefore, a negligence action may not be maintained by Winter (P) against Putnam (D). Affirmed.

EDITOR'S ANALYSIS: This decision is in accord with the rulings in most jurisdictions. See Alm v. Nostrand Reinhold Co., Inc., 480 N.E. 2d 1263 (Ill. 1985). The court also stated that since the publisher is not a guarantor of the accuracy of an author's statements, an action for negligent misrepresentation could not be maintained. The elements of negligent misrepresentation are stated in § 311 of the Restatement (Second) of Torts.

[For more information on misrepresentation, see Casenote Law Outline on Torts, Chapter 12, § III, Negligent Misrepresentation.]

NOTE TO THE STUDENT

OUR GOAL. It is the goal of Casenotes Publishing Company, Inc. to create and distribute the finest, clearest and most accurate legal briefs available. To this end, we are constantly seeking new ideas, comments and constructive criticism. As a user of *Casenote Legal Briefs,* your suggestions will be highly valued. With all correspondence, please include your complete name, address, and telephone number, including area code and zip code.

THE TOTAL STUDY SYSTEM. Casenote Legal Briefs are just one part of the Casenotes TOTAL STUDY SYSTEM. Most briefs are (wherever possible) cross-referenced to the appropriate *Casenote Law Outline,* which will elaborate on the issue at hand. By purchasing a Law Outline together with your Legal Brief, you will have both parts of the Casenotes TOTAL STUDY SYSTEM. (See the advertising in the front of this book for a list of Law Outlines currently available.)

A NOTE ABOUT LANGUAGE. Please note that the language used in *Casenote Legal Briefs* in reference to minority groups and women reflects terminology used within the historical context of the time in which the respective courts wrote the opinions. We at Casenotes Publishing Co., Inc. are well aware of and very sensitive to the desires of all people to be treated with dignity and to be referred to as they prefer. Because such preferences change from time to time, and because the language of the courts reflects the time period in which opinions were written, our case briefs will not necessarily reflect contemporary references. We appreciate your understanding and invite your comments.

EDITOR'S NOTE. Casenote Legal Briefs are intended to supplement the student's casebook, not replace it. There is no substitute for the student's own mastery of this important learning and study technique. If used properly, *Casenote Legal Briefs* are an effective law study aid that will serve to reinforce the student's understanding of the cases.

Casenote™ Legal Briefs

Copyright

Adaptable to courses utilizing **Goldstein's** casebook on Copyright

1999 NEW EDITION SUPPLEMENT *

TABLE OF CASES

*This supplement contains briefs of major cases not included in the previous edition(s) of the casebook or in any paperback supplement to that casebook. If you find any cases are missing, they may have appeared in earlier *Casenote* supplements. To obtain a complimentary copy of these supplements, please use the **SUPPLEMENT REQUEST FORM** located in the bound *Casenote Legal Briefs* adaptable to the casebook in question, being certain to **FOLLOW THE PRINTED INSTRUCTIONS.** This will bring your primary *Casenote* volume completely up to date, if it is not already.

PUBLISHED BY **CASENOTES PUBLISHING CO., INC. 1640 5th ST., SUITE 208, SANTA MONICA, CA 90401**

WARNER-JENKINSON COMPANY, INC. v. HILTON DAVIS CHEMICAL CO.

Alleged infringer (D) v. Patent owner (P)

520 U.S. 17 (1997).

NATURE OF CASE: Appeal from a finding of patent infringement and an order for a permanent injunction.

FACT SUMMARY: When accused of patent infringement, Warner-Jenkinson (D) alleged that the doctrine of equivalents had been overruled.

CONCISE RULE OF LAW: The doctrine of equivalents must be applied to individual elements of the claim, and not to the invention as a whole.

FACTS: Hilton Davis (P) held a patent on an untrafiltration process for removing impurities from manufactured dyes. Hilton Davis (P) sued Warner-Jenkinson (D) for patent infringement, relying on the doctrine of equivalents since there was no literal infringement. Over Warner-Jenkinson's (D) objection that the doctrine of equivalents was an equitable doctrine to be applied by the court, the issue of equivalence was among those sent to the jury. The jury found infringement but, since Warner-Jenkinson (D) had not intentionally infringed, awarded only 20% of the damages sought by Hilton Davis (P). The district court denied Warner Jenkinson's (D) post-trial motions and affirmed, entering a permanent injunction prohibiting Warner-Jenkinson (D) from practicing ultrafiltration below 9.01 pH. A fractured en banc Court of Appeals for the Federal Circuit affirmed, holding that the question of equivalence is for the jury to decide and that the jury in this case had substantial evidence from which it could conclude that the Warner-Jenkinson (D) process was not substantially different from the ultrafiltration process disclosed in Hilton Davis' (P) '746 patent. Warner-Jenkinson (D) appealed, and the Supreme Court granted certiorari.

ISSUE: Must the doctrine of equivalents be applied to individual elements of the claim, and not to the invention as a whole?

HOLDING AND DECISION: (Thomas, J.) Yes. The doctrine of equivalents must be applied to individual elements of the claim, and not to the invention as a whole. The accused device or practice must be more than equivalent overall. When applied broadly, the doctrine of equivalents conflicts with the definitional and public-notice functions of the statutory claiming requirement. The lengthy history of the doctrine of equivalents strongly supports adherence to our refusal in Grover Tank & Mfg. Company. v. Linde Air Products Company., 339 U.S. 605, to find that the 1952 Patent Act conflicts with that doctrine. Intent plays no role in the application of the doctrine of equivalents. The proper time for evaluating equivalency is at the time of infringement, not at the time the patent was issued. It is a rule of patent construction that a claim in a patent as allowed must be read and interpreted with reference to claims that have been cancelled or rejected, and the claims cannot by construction be read to cover what was thus eliminated from the patent. Prosecution history estoppel is available as a defense to infringement, but if the patent-holder demonstrates that an amendment required during prosecution had a purpose unrelated to patentability, a court must consider that purpose in order to decide whether an estoppel is precluded. Where the patentholder is unable to establish such a purpose, a court should presume that the purpose behind the required amendment is such that prosecution history estoppel would apply. Reversed and remanded.

CONCURRENCE: (Ginsberg, J.) The new rebuttable presumption regarding prosecution history estoppel, if applied woodenly, might in some instances unfairly discount the expectations of a patentee who had no notice at the time of patent prosecution that such a presumption would apply. Years after the fact, the patentee may find it difficult to establish an evidentiary basis that would overcome the new presumption. On remand, the Federal Circuit Court can determine - bearing in mind the prior absence of clear rules of the game - whether suitable reasons for including the lower pH limit were earlier offered or, if not, whether they can now be established.

EDITOR'S ANALYSIS: Prosecution history estoppel is also known as file wrapper estopple. It differs from common law estoppel in that the accused infringer need not prove reliance as an element of the estoppel. If an inventor adopts a narrow definition in the Patent and Trademark Office in order to obtain a patent, he may not later rely upon a broader definition in an infringement suit.

SELLE v. GIBB

Copyright owner (P) v. Alleged infringer (D)

741 F.2d 896 (7th Cir. 1997).

NATURE OF CASE: Appeal from a judgment notwithstanding the verdict.

FACT SUMMARY: Selle (P) alleged there the the Gibb brothers (D), known as the Bee Gees, had infringed the copyright of his song.

CONCISE RULE OF LAW: Inference of access giving rise to copyright infringement may not be based on mere conjecture, speculation or a bare possibility of access.

FACTS: Selle (P) composed a song in 1975 and obtained a copyright for it later that year. He played his song with his small band two or three times in Chicago and sent a tape of the music to eleven music recording and publishing companies. Eight of the companies returned the materials and three did not respond. When Selle (P) heard the Bee Gees' (D) song "How Deep Is Your Love," in 1978, he thought he recognized the music as his own, although the lyrics were different. When Selle (P) sued for infringement, Gibb (D) and the Bee Gees presented testimony that they had independently composed their song. Although Selle (P) presented evidence that the two songs were substantially similar, there was no direct evidence of access. The jury returned a verdict in Selle's (P) favor on the issue of liability in a bifurcated trial. The district court judge granted Gibb's (D) motion for judgment notwithstanding the verdict and, in the alternative for a new trial. Selle (P) appealed.

ISSUE: May inference of access giving rise to copyright infringement be based on mere conjecture, speculation or a bare possibility of access?

HOLDING AND DECISION: (Cudahy, J.) No. Inference of access giving rise to copyright infringement may not be based on mere conjecture, speculation or a bare possibility of access. The judge's conclusions that there was no more than a bare possibility that Gibbs (D) could have had access to Selle's (P) song and that this was an insufficient basis from which the jury could have reasonably inferred the existence of access seem correct. Although proof of striking similarity may permit an inference of access, Selle (P) must still meet some minimum threshold of proof which demonstrates that the inference of access is reasonable. In this case, the availability of Selle's (P) song was virtually de minimis. In order to bolster the expert's conclusion that independent creation was not possible, there should be some testimony or other evidence of the relative complexity or uniqueness of the two compositions. The evidence of striking similarity was not sufficiently compelling to make the case when the proof of access must otherwise depend largely upon speculation and conjecture. Affirmed.

Continued on next page

EDITOR'S ANALYSIS: To establish a claim of copyright infringement of a musical composition, the plaintiff must prove ownership of a copyright, originality of the work, copying of the work by the defendant, and a substantial degree of similarity between the two works. The third element was at issue in this case. If the plaintiff presents evidence of striking similarity sufficient to raise an inference of access, then copying is presumably proved simultaneously.

QUICKNOTES

COPYRIGHT - Refers to the exclusive rights granted to an artist pursuant to Article I, section 8, clause 8 of the United States Constitution over the reproduction, display, performance, distribution, and adaptation of his work for a period prescribed by statute.

DE MINIMIS - Insignificant; trivial; not of sufficient significance to resort to legal action.

STATE STREET BANK & TRUST COMPANY. v. SIGNATURE FINANCIAL GROUP, INC.

Competitor (P) v. Patent owner (D)

149 F.3d 1368 (Federal. Cir. 1998).

NATURE OF CASE: Appeal from summary judgment of patent invalidity for plaintiff.

FACT SUMMARY: When Signature's (D) patent for a system monitoring and recording financial information flow was held to be invalid for failure to claim statutory matter, an appeal followed.

CONCISE RULE OF LAW: To be patentable, an abstract formula, algorithm, or calculation must be applied in a practical way that produces a useful, concrete, and tangible result

FACTS: Signature (D) was the assignee of a patent entitled "Data Processing System for Hub and Spoke Financial Services Configuration." The system facilitated a structure whereby mutual funds (Spokes) pooled their assets in an investment portfolio (Hub) organized as a partnership. State Street (P) and Signature (D) both act as custodians and accounting agents for multi-tiered partnership fund financial services. State Street (P) negotiated with Signature (D) for a license to use its patented data processing system, but when negotiations broke down, it sought a declaratory judgment asserting invalidity, unenforceability, and noninfringement. The district court granted State Street's (P) motion for partial summary judgment of patent invalidity for failure to claim statutory subject matter under 35 U.S.C. § 101. Signature (D) appealed.

ISSUE: To be patentable, must an abstract formula, algorithm, or calculation be applied in a practical way that produces a useful, concrete, and tangible result?

HOLDING AND DECISION: (Stevens, J.) Yes. To be patentable, an abstract formula, algorithm, or calculation must be applied in a practical way that produces a useful, concrete, and tangible result. The transformation of an abstraction such as data, representing discrete dollar amounts, by a machine through a series of mathematical calculations into a final share price, constitutes a practical application of a mathematical algorithm, formula or calculation, because it produces a useful, concrete, and tangible result. The district court erred by applying the Freeman-Walter-Abele test to determine whether the claimed subject matter was an unpatentable abstract idea. The mere fact that a claimed invention involves inputting numbers, calculating numbers, outputting numbers, and storing numbers, in and of itself, would not render it nonstatutory subject matter, unless its operation did not produce a useful, concrete, and tangible result. The district court erred in concluding that the claimed subject matter fell into one of two judicially-created exceptions to statutory subject matter. Neither the "mathematical algorithm" exception nor the "business method" exception apply to this case. Since the 1952 Patent Act, business methods have been, and should have been, subject to the same legal requirements for patentability as applied to any other process or method. Whether the claims are directed to subject matter within § 101 should not turn on whether the claimed subject matter does "business" instead of something else. Reversed and remanded.

EDITOR'S ANALYSIS: The court in this case laid to rest the "business method" exception. Earlier cases rejecting claimed inventions as abstract ideas under the "mathematical algorithm" exception referred to the "business methods" exception, but the most recent edition of the Manual of Patent Examining Procedures (1996) states that relevant claims should not be categorized as methods of doing business. Instead such claims should be treated like any other process claims. Computer software used for business applications are now patentable, reversing earlier decisions.

QUICKNOTES

35 U.S.C. 101 - Any new and useful process, machine, manufacture, or composition of matter, or any new and useful improvement thereof is patentable.

the Ultimate Outline

- *RENOWNED AUTHORS: Every **Casenote Law Outline** is written by highly respected, nationally recognized professors.*
- *KEYED TO **CASENOTE LEGAL BRIEF** BOOKS: In most cases, **Casenote Law Outlines** work in conjunction with the **Casenote Legal Briefs** so that you can see how each case in your textbook relates to the entire subject area. In addition, **Casenote Law Outlines** are cross-referenced to most major casebooks.*
- *FREE SUPPLEMENT SERVICE: As part of being the most up-to-date legal outline on the market, whenever a new supplement is published, the corresponding outline can be updated for free using the supplement request form found in this book.*

ADMINISTRATIVE LAW (1996) **$21.95**
Charles H. Koch, Jr., Dudley W. Woodbridge Professor of Law, College of William and Mary
Sidney A. Shapiro, John M. Rounds Professor of Law, University of Kansas

CIVIL PROCEDURE (1996) **$22.95**
John B. Oakley, Professor of Law, University of California, Davis School of Law
Rex R. Perschbacher, Dean of University of California, Davis School of Law

COMMERCIAL LAW (see SALES ● SECURED TRANSACTIONS ● NEGOTIABLE INSTRUMENTS & PAYMENT SYSTEMS)

CONFLICT OF LAWS (1996) **$21.95**
Luther L. McDougal, III, W.R. Irby Professor of Law, Tulane University
Robert L. Felix, James P. Mozingo, III, Professor of Law, University of South Carolina

CONSTITUTIONAL LAW (1997) **$24.95**
Gary Goodpaster, Professor of Law, University of California, Davis School of Law

CONTRACTS (1996) **$21.95**
Daniel Wm. Fessler, Professor of Law, University of California, Davis School of Law

CORPORATIONS (1997) **$24.95**
Lewis D. Solomon, Arthur Selwin Miller Research Professor of Law, George Washington University
Daniel Wm. Fessler, Professor of Law, University of California, Davis School of Law
Arthur E. Wilmarth, Jr., Associate Professor of Law, George Washington University

CRIMINAL LAW (1996) **$21.95**
Joshua Dressler, Professor of Law, McGeorge School of Law

CRIMINAL PROCEDURE (1997) **$20.95**
Joshua Dressler, Professor of Law, McGeorge School of Law

ESTATE & GIFT TAX **$21.95**
Joseph M. Dodge, W.H. Francis Professor of Law, University of Texas at Austin

EVIDENCE (1996) **$23.95**
Kenneth Graham, Jr., Professor of Law, University of California, Los Angeles

FEDERAL COURTS (1997) **$22.95**
Howard P. Fink, Isadore and Ida Topper Professor of Law, Ohio State University
Linda S. Mullenix, Bernard J. Ward Centennial Professor of Law, University of Texas

FEDERAL INCOME TAXATION (1998) **$22.95**
Joseph M. Dodge, W.H. Francis Professor of Law, University of Texas at Austin

LEGAL RESEARCH (1996) **$21.95**
Nancy L. Schultz, Professor of Law, Chapman University
Louis J. Sirico, Jr., Professor of Law, Villanova University

NEGOTIABLE INSTRUMENTS & PAYMENT SYSTEMS (1995) **$22.95**
Donald B. King, Professor of Law, Saint Louis University
Peter Winship, James Cleo Thompson, Sr. Trustee Professor, SMU

PROPERTY (1997) **$22.95**
Sheldon F. Kurtz, Percy Bordwell Professor of Law, University of Iowa
Patricia Cain, Professor of Law, University of Iowa

SALES **$21.95**
Robert E. Scott, Dean and Lewis F. Powell, Jr. Professor of Law, University of Virginia
Donald B. King, Professor of Law, Saint Louis University

SECURED TRANSACTIONS (1995 w/ '96 supp.) **$20.95**
Donald B. King, Professor of Law, Saint Louis University

TORTS (1996) **$22.95**
George C. Christie, James B. Duke Professor of Law, Duke University
Jerry J. Phillips, W.P. Toms Professor of Law, University of Tennessee

WILLS, TRUSTS, & ESTATES (1996) **$22.95**
William M. McGovern, Professor of Law, University of California, Los Angeles

REF. # 1502-93-296

SUPPLEMENT REQUEST FORM

At the time this book was printed, a brief was included for every major case in the casebook and for every existing supplement to the casebook. However, if a new supplement to the casebook (or a new edition of the casebook) has been published since this publication was printed and if that casebook supplement (or new edition of the casebook) was available for sale at the time you purchased this Casenote Legal Briefs book, we will be pleased to provide you the new cases contained therein AT NO CHARGE when you send us a stamped, self-addressed envelope.

TO OBTAIN YOUR FREE SUPPLEMENT MATERIAL, **YOU MUST FOLLOW THE INSTRUCTIONS BELOW PRECISELY** OR YOUR REQUEST WILL NOT BE ACKNOWLEDGED!

1. Please check if there is in fact an existing supplement and, if so, that the cases are not already included in your Casenote Legal Briefs. Check the main table of cases as well as the supplement table of cases, if any.
2. **REMOVE THIS ENTIRE PAGE FROM THE BOOK.** You MUST send this ORIGINAL page to receive your supplement. This page acts as your proof of purchase and contains the reference number necessary to fill your supplement request properly. No photocopy of this page or written request will be honored or answered. Any request from which the reference number has been removed, altered or obliterated will not be honored.
3. ✶ Prepare a STAMPED self-addressed envelope for return mailing. Be sure to use a FULL SIZE (9 X 12) ENVELOPE (MANILA TYPE) so that the supplement will fit and AFFIX ENOUGH POSTAGE TO COVER 3 OZ. **ANY SUPPLEMENT REQUEST NOT ACCOMPANIED BY A STAMPED SELF-ADDRESSED ENVELOPE WILL ABSOLUTELY NOT BE FILLED OR ACKNOWLEDGED.**
4. MULTIPLE SUPPLEMENT REQUESTS: If you are ordering more than one supplement, we suggest that you enclose a stamped, self-addressed envelope for each supplement requested. If you enclose only one envelope for a multiple request, your order may not be filled immediately should any supplement which you requested still be in production. In other words, your order will be held by us until it can be filled completely.
5. Casenotes prints two kinds of supplements. A "New Edition" supplement is issued when a new edition of your casebook is published. A "New Edition" supplement gives you all major cases found in the new edition of the casebook which did not appear in the previous edition. A regular "supplement" is issued when a paperback supplement to your casebook is published. If the box at the lower right is stamped, then the "New Edition" supplement was provided to your bookstore and is *not* available from Casenotes; however, Casenotes will still send you any regular "supplements" which have been printed either before or after the new edition of your casebook appeared and which, according to the reference number at the top of this page, have not been included in this book. If the box is not stamped, Casenotes will send you any supplements, "New Edition" and/or regular, needed to completely update your Casenote Legal Briefs.

✶☞ ***NOTE:*** **REQUESTS FOR SUPPLEMENTS WILL NOT BE FILLED UNLESS THESE INSTRUCTIONS ARE COMPLIED WITH!**

6. Fill in the following information:

Full title of CASEBOOK **COPYRIGHT**

CASEBOOK author's name **Goldstein**

Date of new supplement you are requesting ______

Name and location of bookstore where this Casenote Legal Brief was purchased ______

Name and location of law school you attend ______

Any comments regarding Casenote Legal Briefs ______

LATEST NEW EDITION ...

NOTE: IF THIS BOX IS STAMPED, NO NEW EDITION SUPPLEMENT CAN BE OBTAINED BY MAIL.

PUBLISHED BY CASENOTES PUBLISHING CO., INC. 1640 5th ST, SUITE 208 SANTA MONICA, CA 90401

PLEASE PRINT

NAME ______ **PHONE** ______ **DATE** ______

ADDRESS/CITY/STATE/ZIP ______

Announcing the First *Totally Integrated* Law Study System

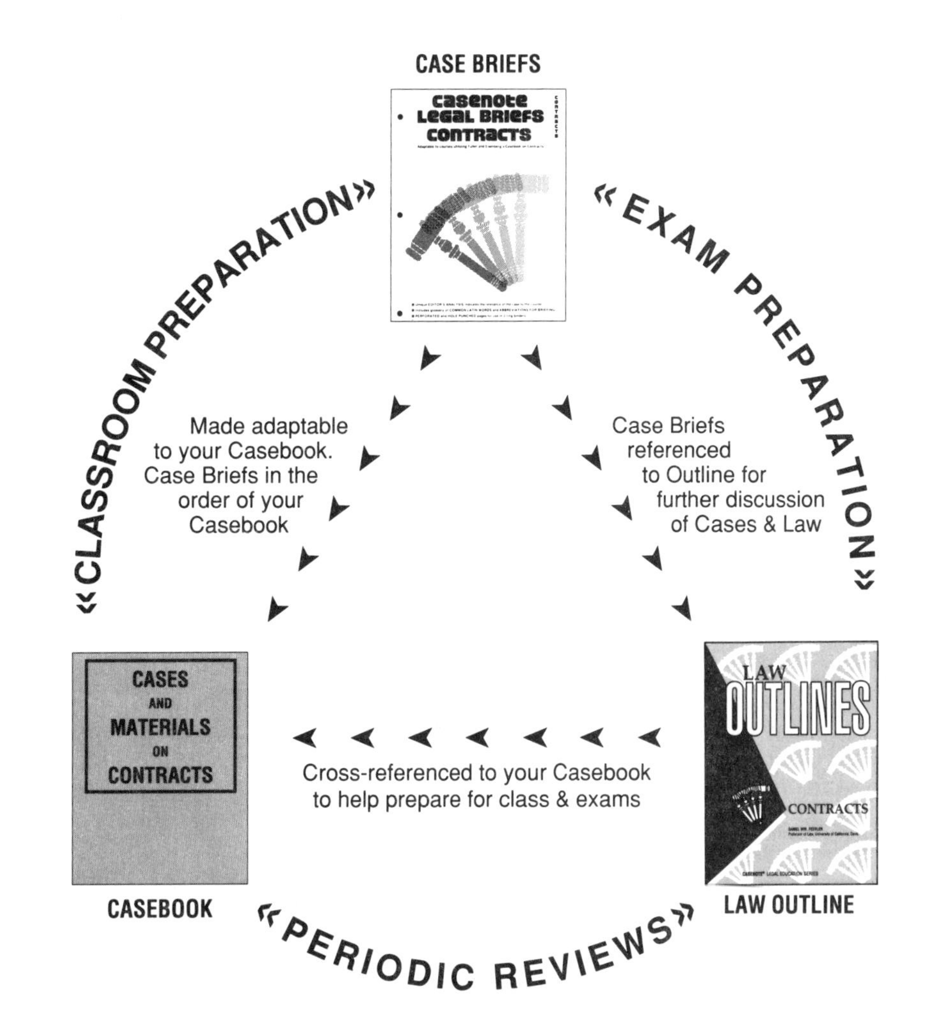

Casenotes Integrated Study System Makes Studying Easier and More Effective Than Ever!

Casenotes has just made studying easier and more effective than ever before, because we've done the work for you! Through our exclusive integrated study system, most briefs found in this volume of Casenote Legal Briefs are cross-referenced to the corresponding area of law in the Casenote Law Outline series. The cross-reference immediately follows the Editor's Analysis at the end of the brief, and it will direct you to the corresponding chapter and section number in the Casenote Law Outline for further information on the case or the area of law.

This cross-referencing feature will enable you to make the most effective use of your time. While each Casenote Law Outline focuses on a particular subject area of the law, each legal briefs volume is adapted to a specific casebook. Now, with cross-referencing of Casenote Legal Briefs to Casenote Law Outlines, you can have the best of both worlds – briefs for all major cases in your casebooks and easy-to-find, easy-to-read explanations of the law in our Law Outline series. Casenote Law Outlines are authored exclusively by law professors who are nationally recognized authorities in their field. So using Casenote Law Outlines is like studying with the top law professors.

Try Casenotes new totally integrated study system and see just how easy and effective studying can be.

Casenotes Integrated Study System Does The Work For You!

CASENOTE™ LEGAL BRIEFS

PRICE LIST — EFFECTIVE JULY 1, 1996 ● PRICES SUBJECT TO CHANGE WITHOUT NOTICE

Ref. No.	Course	Adaptable to Courses Utilizing	Retail Price
1265	ADMINISTRATIVE LAW	BONFIELD & ASIMOV	16.00
1263	ADMINISTRATIVE LAW	BREYER & STEWART	18.00
1266	ADMINISTRATIVE LAW	CASS, DIVER & BEERMAN	TBA
1260	ADMINISTRATIVE LAW	GELLHORN, B., S., R., S. & F.	16.00
1264	ADMINISTRATIVE LAW	MASHAW, MERRILL & SHANE	17.50
1262	ADMINISTRATIVE LAW	SCHWARTZ	17.00
1290	ADMIRALTY	HEALY & SHARPE	20.00
1291	ADMIRALTY	LUCAS	17.50
1350	AGENCY & PARTNERSHIP (ENT.ORG)	CONARD, KNAUSS & SIEGEL	20.00
1351	AGENCY & PARTNERSHIP	HYNES	19.00
1281	ANTITRUST (TRADE REGULATION)	HANDLER, B. P. & G.	16.50
1283	ANTITRUST	SULLIVAN & HOVENKAMP	17.00
1611	BANKING LAW	MACEY & MILLER	16.00
1610	BANKING LAW	SYMONS & WHITE	14.00
1303	BANKRUPTCY (DEBTOR-CREDITOR)	EISENBERG	18.00
1440	BUSINESS PLANNING	HERWITZ	12.50
1040	CIVIL PROCEDURE	COUND, F., M. & S	19.00
1043	CIVIL PROCEDURE	FIELD, KAPLAN & CLERMONT	19.00
1041	CIVIL PROCEDURE	HAZARD, TAIT & FLETCHER	18.00
1047	CIVIL PROCEDURE	MARCUS, REDISH & SHERMAN	18.00
1044	CIVIL PROCEDURE	ROSENBERG, S. & D.	19.00
1046	CIVIL PROCEDURE	YEAZELL, LANDERS, & MARTI6	16.00
1311	COMM'L LAW	FARNSWORTH, H., R., H. & 7.	18.00
1312	COMM'L LAW	JORDAN & WARREN	18.00
1310	COMM'L LAW (SALES/SEC.TR./PAY.LAW)	SPEIDEL, SUMMERS & WHITE	20.00
1313	COMM'L LAW (SALES/SEC.TR./PAY.LAW)	WHALEY	17.00
1320	COMMUNITY PROPERTY	BIRD	16.50
1630	COMPARATIVE LAW	SCHLESINGER, B., D., & H.	15.00
1048	COMPLEX LITIGATION	MARCUS & SHERMAN	16.00
1072	CONFLICTS	BRILMAYER	16.00
1071	CONFLICTS	CRAMTON, CURRIE & KAY	16.00
1070	CONFLICTS	REESE, ROSENBERG & HAY	19.00
1086	CONSTITUTIONAL LAW	BREST & LEVINSON	17.00
1082	CONSTITUTIONAL LAW	COHEN & VARAT	20.00
1088	CONSTITUTIONAL LAW	FARBER, ESKRIDGE & FRICKEY	17.00
1080	CONSTITUTIONAL LAW	GUNTHER	18.00
1081	CONSTITUTIONAL LAW	LOCKHART, K., C. & S.	17.00
1085	CONSTITUTIONAL LAW	ROTUNDA	19.00
1087	CONSTITUTIONAL LAW	STONE, S., S. & T.	18.00
1017	CONTRACTS	CALAMARI, PERILLO & BENDER	22.00
1101	CONTRACTS	CRANDALL & WHALEY	19.00
1014	CONTRACTS	DAWSON, HARVEY & HENDRESON	18.00
1010	CONTRACTS	FARNSWORTH & YOUNG	17.00
1011	CONTRACTS	FULLER & EISENBERG	19.00
1100	CONTRACTS	HAMILTON, RAU & WEINTRAUB	18.00
1013	CONTRACTS	KESSLER, GILMORE & KRONMAN	22.00
1016	CONTRACTS	KNAPP & CRYSTAL	19.50
1012	CONTRACTS	MURPHY & SPEIDEL	21.00
1018	CONTRACTS	MURRAY	21.00
1015	CONTRACTS	ROSETT	20.00
1019	CONTRACTS	VERNON	19.00
1502	COPYRIGHT	GOLDSTEIN	17.00
1501	COPYRIGHT	NIMMER, M., M., & N.	18.50
1218	CORPORATE TAXATION	LIND, S. L. & R	13.00
1050	CORPORATIONS	CARY & EISENBERG (ABR. & UNA8R.)	18.00
1054	CORPORATIONS	CHOPER, MORRIS & COFFEE	20.50
1350	CORPORATIONS (ENTERPRISE ORG.)	CONARD, KNAUSS & SIEGEL	20.00
1053	CORPORATIONS	HAMILTON	18.00
1057	CORPORATIONS	O'KELLEY & THOMPSON	17.00
1056	CORPORATIONS	SOLOMON, S., B., & W.	18.00
1052	CORPORATIONS	VAGTS	16.00
1300	CREDITOR'S RIGHTS (DEBTOR-CREDITOR)	RIESENFELD	20.00
1550	CRIMINAL JUSTICE	WEINREB	17.00
1020	CRIMINAL LAW	BOYCE & PERKINS	21.00
1024	CRIMINAL LAW	DIX & SHARLOT	16.00
1028	CRIMINAL LAW	DRESSLER	20.00
1027	CRIMINAL LAW	JOHNSON	19.00
1021	CRIMINAL LAW	KADISH & SCHULHOFER	18.00
1026	CRIMINAL LAW	KAPLAN & WEISBERG	17.00
1023	CRIMINAL LAW	LAFAVE	18.00
1022	CRIMINAL LAW	WEINREB	14.00
1205	CRIMINAL PROCEDURE	ALLEN, KUHNS & STUNTZ	16.00
1202	CRIMINAL PROCEDURE	HADDAD, Z., S. & B.	19.00
1200	CRIMINAL PROCEDURE	KAMISAR, LAFAVE & ISRAEL	18.00
1204	CRIMINAL PROCEDURE	SALTZBURG & CAPRA	16.00
1203	CRIMINAL PROCEDURE (PROCESS)	WEINREB	17.50
1303	DEBTOR-CREDITOR	EISENBERG	18.00
1302	DEBTOR-CREDITOR	EPSTEIN, LANDERS & NICKLES	17.00
1300	DEBTOR-CREDITOR (CRED. RTS.)	RIESENFELD	20.00
1304	DEBTOR-CREDITOR	WARREN & WESTBROOK	18.00
1224	DECEDENTS ESTATES	RITCHIE, ALFORD, EFFLAND & DORIS	20.00
1222	DECEDENTS ESTATES	SCOLES & HALBACH	20.50
1231	DECEDENTS ESTATES (TRUSTS)	WAGGONER, WELLMAN, A. & F.	19.00
	DOMESTIC RELATIONS (*see* **FAMILY LAW**)		
1690	EDUCATION LAW	YUDOF, KIRP & LEVIN	TBA
1670	EMPLOYMENT DISCRIMINATION	FRIEDMAN & STRICKLER	16.00
1671	EMPLOYMENT DISCRIMINATION	ZIMMER, SULLIVAN, R. & C.	17.00
1660	EMPLOYMENT LAW	ROTHSTEIN, KNAPP & LIEBMAN	18.50
1350	ENTERPRISE ORGANIZATION	CONARD, KNAUSS & SIEGEL	20.00
1342	ENVIRONMENTAL LAW	ANDERSON, MANDELKER & TARLOCK	15.00
1341	ENVIRONMENTAL LAW	FINDLEY & FARBER	17.00
1345	ENVIRONMENTAL LAW	MENELL & STEWART	TBA
1344	ENVIRONMENTAL LAW	PERCIVAL, MILLER, S. & L.	17.00
1343	ENVIRONMENTAL LAW	PLATER, ABRAMS & GOLDFARB	16.00
	EQUITY (*see* **REMEDIES**)		
1217	ESTATE & GIFT TAXATION	BITTKER & CLARK	14.00
1214	ESTATE & GIFT TAXATION	KAHN & WAGGONER	16.00
1213	ESTATE & GIFT TAX (FED. WEALTH TRANS.)	SURREY, MCDANIEL & GUTMAN	15.00
	ETHICS (*see* **PROFESSIONAL RESPONSIBILITY**)		
1065	EVIDENCE	GREEN & NESSON	19.00
1063	EVIDENCE	LEMPERT & SALTZBURG	11.00
1066	EVIDENCE	MUELLER & KIRKPATRICK	16.00
1064	EVIDENCE	STRONG, BROUN & MOUSTELLER	21.50
1062	EVIDENCE	SUTTON & WELLBORN	21.00
1061	EVIDENCE	WALTZ & PARK	19.00
1060	EVIDENCE	WEINSTEIN, M., A. & B.	21.50
1244	FAMILY LAW (DOMESTIC RELATION)	AREEN	21.00
1242	FAMILY LAW (DOMESTIC RELATION)	CLARK & GLOWINSKY	18.00
1245	FAMILY LAW (DOMESTIC RELATION)	ELLMAN, KURTZ & BARTLETT	19.00
1243	FAMILY LAW (DOMESTIC RELATION)	KRAUSE	23.00
1240	FAMILY LAW (DOMESTIC RELATION)	WADLINGTON	19.00
1231	FAMILY PROPERTY LAW (WILLS/TRUSTS)	WAGGONER, WELLMAN, A. & F.	19.00
1360	FEDERAL COURTS	BATOR ET AL. (HART & WECHSLER)	18.00
1362	FEDERAL COURTS	CURRIE	16.00
1363	FEDERAL COURTS	LOW & JEFFRIES	15.00
1361	FEDERAL COURTS	MCCORMICK, C. & W.	19.00
1364	FEDERAL COURTS	REDISH & NICHOL	16.00
1510	GRATUITOUS TRANSFERS	CLARK, LUSKY & MURPHY	17.00
1650	HEALTH LAW	FURROW, J., J., & S.	16.50
1640	IMMIGRATION LAW	ALEINIKOFF, MARTIN & MOTOMURA	15.00
1371	INSURANCE LAW	KEETON	20.00
1372	INSURANCE LAW	YORK, WHELAN & MARTINEZ	18.00
1370	INSURANCE LAW	YOUNG & HOLMES	16.00
1394	INTERNATIONAL BUSINESS TRANSACTIONS	FOLSOM, GORDON & SPANOGLE	14.00
1393	INTERNATIONAL LAW	CARTER & TRIMBLE	15.00
1392	INTERNATIONAL LAW	HENKIN, P., S. & S.	16.00
1390	INTERNATIONAL LAW	OLIVER, F., B., S., & W.	21.00
1331	LABOR LAW	COX, BOK, GORMAN & FINKIN	18.00
1333	LABOR LAW	LESLIE	17.50
1332	LABOR LAW	MELTZER & HENDERSON	19.00
1330	LABOR LAW	MERRIFIELD, S. & C.	18.00
1471	LAND FINANCE (REAL ESTATE TRANS)	BERGER & JOHNSTONE	17.00
1620	LAND FINANCE (REAL ESTATE TRANS)	NELSON & WHITMAN	18.00
1470	LAND FINANCE	PENNEY, B. & C.	15.00
1451	LAND USE	CALLIES, FREILICH & ROBERTS	TBA
1450	LAND USE	WRIGHT & GITELMAN	22.00
1421	LEGISLATION	ESKRIDGE & FRICKEY	14.00
1590	LOCAL GOVERNMENT LAW	VALENTE & McCARTHY	21.00
1480	MASS MEDIA	FRANKLIN & ANDERSON	14.00
1312	NEGOTIABLE INSTRUMENTS (COMM. LAW)	JORDAN & WARREN	18.00
1313	NEGOTIABLE INSTRUMENTS (COMM. LAW)	WHALEY	17.00
1570	NEW YORK PRACTICE	PETERFREUND & McLAUGHLIN	24.00
1541	OIL & GAS	KUNTZ, L., A. & S.	17.00
1540	OIL & GAS	MAXWELL, WILLIAMS, M. & K.	17.00
1560	PATENT LAW	FRANCIS & COLLINS (CHOATE)	22.00
1310	PAYMENT LAW (COMM LAW, SALES & SEC.TR.)	SPEIDEL, SUMMERS & WHITE	20.00
1313	PAYMENT LAW (COMM.LAW / NEG. INST.)	WHALEY	17.00
1431	PRODUCTS LIABILITY	KEETON, O., M., & G.	19.00
1091	PROF. RESPONSIBILITY (ETHICS)	GILLERS	12.00
1093	PROF. RESPONSIBILITY (ETHICS)	HAZARD, KONIAK, & CRAMTON	17.00
1092	PROF. RESPONSIBILITY (ETHICS)	MORGAN & ROTUNDA	12.00
1033	PROPERTY	BROWDER, C., N., S.& W.	19.50
1030	PROPERTY	CASNER & LEACH	20.00
1031	PROPERTY	CRIBBET, JOHNSON, FINLEY & SMITH	20.50
1037	PROPERTY	DONAHUE, KAUPER & MARTIN	17.00
1035	PROPERTY	DUKEMINIER & KRIER	17.00
1034	PROPERTY	HAAR & LIEBMAN	19.50
1036	PROPERTY	KURTZ & HOVENKAMP	18.00
1032	PROPERTY	RABIN & KWALL	19.00
1038	PROPERTY	SINGER	TBA
1621	REAL ESTATE TRANSACTIONS	GOLDSTEIN & KORNGOLD	17.00
1471	REAL ESTATE TRANS. & FIN. (LAND FINANCE)	BERGER & JOHNSTONE	16.00
1620	REAL ESTATE TRANSFER & FINANCE	NELSON & WHITMAN	17.00
1254	REMEDIES (EQUITY)	LAYCOCK	19.00
1253	REMEDIES (EQUITY)	LEAVELL, L., N. & K/F.	20.00
1252	REMEDIES (EQUITY)	RE & RE	22.00
1255	REMEDIES (EQUITY)	SHOBEN & TABB	21.50
1250	REMEDIES (EQUITY)	YORK, BAUMAN & RENDLEMAN	24.00
1312	SALES (COMM. LAW)	JORDAN & WARREN	18.00
1310	SALES (COMM. LAW)	SPEIDEL, SUMMERS & WHITE	20.00
1313	SALES (COMM. LAW)	WHALEY	17.00
1312	SECURED TRANS. (COMM. LAW)	JORDAN & WARREN	18.00
1310	SECURED TRANS.	SPEIDEL, SUMMERS & WHITE	20.00
1313	SECURED TRANS. (COMM. LAW)	WHALEY	17.00
1272	SECURITIES REGULATION	COX, HILLMAN, LANGEVOORT	17.00
1270	SECURITIES REGULATION	JENNINGS, MARSH & COFFEE	17.00
1271	SECURITIES REGULATION	RATNER	17.00
1680	SPORTS LAW	WEILER & ROBERTS	16.50
1215	TAXATION (BASIC FED. INC.)	ANDREWS	20.00
1217	TAXATION (ESTATE & GIFT)	BITTKER & CLARK	14.00
1212	TAXATION (FED. INC.)	FREELAND, LIND & STEPHENS	17.00
1211	TAXATION (FED. INC.)	GRAETZ & SCHENK	16.00
1214	TAXATION (ESTATE & GIFT)	KAHN & WAGGONER	16.00
1210	TAXATION (FED. INC.)	KLEIN & BANKMAN	17.00
1218	TAXATION (CORPORATE)	LIND, S., L. & R.	13.00
1213	TAXATION (FED. WEALTH TRANS.)	SURREY, MCDANIEL & GUTMAN	15.00
1006	TORTS	DOBBS	18.00
1003	TORTS	EPSTEIN	19.50
1004	TORTS	FRANKLIN & RABIN	16.50
1001	TORTS	HENDERSON, P. & S.	19.50
1002	TORTS	KEETON, K., S. & S.	22.00
1000	TORTS	PROSSER, W., S., K., & P.	23.00
1005	TORTS	SHULMAN, JAMES & GRAY	21.00
1281	TRADE REGULATION (ANTITRUST)	HANDLER, B., P. & G.	16.50
1230	TRUSTS	BOGERT, O., H., & H.	19.50
1231	TRUSTS/WILLS (FAMILY PROPERTY LAW)	WAGGONER, WELLMAN A. & F.	19.00
1410	U.C.C	EPSTEIN, MARTIN, H. & N.	14.00
1580	WATER LAW	TRELEASE & GOULD	18.00
1223	WILLS, TRUSTS & ESTATES	DUKEMINIER & JOHANSON	18.00
1220	WILLS	MECHEM & ATKINSON	19.00
1231	WILLS/TRUSTS (FAMILY PROPERTY LAW)	WAGGONER, WELLMAN A. & F.	19.00

(SERIES XXXIX)

CASENOTES PUBLISHING CO. INC. ● 1640 FIFTH STREET, SUITE 208 ● SANTA MONICA, CA 90401 ● (310) 395-6500

PLEASE PURCHASE FROM YOUR LOCAL BOOKSTORE. IF UNAVAILABLE, YOU MAY ORDER DIRECT.*

4TH CLASS POSTAGE (ALLOW TWO WEEKS) $1.00 PER ORDER; 1ST CLASS POSTAGE $3.00 (ONE BOOK), $2.00 EACH (TWO OR MORE BOOKS)

*CALIF. RESIDENTS PLEASE ADD 8¼% SALES TAX

NOTES

HOW TO BRIEF A CASE

A. DECIDE ON A FORMAT AND STICK TO IT

Structure is essential to a good brief. It enables you to arrange systematically the related parts that are scattered throughout most cases, thus making manageable and understandable what might otherwise seem to be an endless and unfathomable sea of information. There are, of course, an unlimited number of formats that can be utilized. However, it is best to find one that suits your needs and stick to it. Consistency breeds both efficiency and the security that when called upon you will know where to look in your brief for the information you are asked to give.

Any format, as long as it presents the essential elements of a case in an organized fashion, can be used. Experience, however, has led *Casenotes* to develop and utilize the following format because of its logical flow and universal applicability.

NATURE OF CASE: This is a brief statement of the legal character and procedural status of the case (e.g., "Appeal of a burglary conviction").

There are many different alternatives open to a litigant dissatisfied with a court ruling. The key to determining which one has been used is to discover *who is asking this court for what.*

This first entry in the brief should be kept as *short as possible.* The student should use the court's terminology if the student understands it. But since jurisdictions vary as to the titles of pleadings, the best entry is the one that apprises the student of who wants what in this proceeding, not the one that sounds most like the court's language.

CONCISE RULE OF LAW: A statement of the general principle of law that the case illustrates (e.g., "An acceptance that varies any term of the offer is considered a rejection and counteroffer").

Determining the rule of law of a case is a procedure similar to determining the issue of the case. Avoid being fooled by red herrings; there may be a few rules of law mentioned in the case excerpt, but usually only one is *the* rule with which the casebook editor is concerned. The techniques used to locate the issue, described below, may also be utilized to find the rule of law. Generally, your best guide is simply the chapter heading. It is a clue to the point the casebook editor seeks to make and should be kept in mind when reading every case in the respective section.

FACTS: A synopsis of only the essential facts of the case, i.e., those bearing upon or leading up to the issue.

The facts entry should be a short statement of the events and transactions that led one party to initiate legal proceedings against another in the first place. While some cases conveniently state the salient facts at the beginning of the decision, in other instances they will have to be culled from hiding places throughout the text, even from concurring and dissenting opinions. Some of the "facts" will often be in dispute and should be so noted. Conflicting evidence may be briefly pointed up. "Hard" facts must be included. Both must be *relevant* in order to be listed in the facts entry. It is impossible to tell what is relevant until the entire case is read, as the ultimate determination of the rights and liabilities of the parties may turn on something buried deep in the opinion.

The facts entry should never be longer than one to three *short* sentences.

It is often helpful to identify the role played by a party in a given context. For example, in a construction contract case the identification of a party as the "contractor" or "builder" alleviates the need to tell that that party was the one who was supposed to have built the house.

It is always helpful, and a good general practice, to identify the "plaintiff" and the "defendant." This may seem elementary and uncomplicated, but, especially in view of the creative editing practiced by some casebook editors, it is sometimes a difficult or even impossible task. Bear in mind that the *party presently* seeking something from this court may not be the plaintiff, and that sometimes only the cross-claim of a defendant is treated in the excerpt. Confusing or misaligning the parties can ruin your analysis and understanding of the case.

ISSUE: A statement of the general legal question answered by or illustrated in the case. For clarity, the issue is best put in the form of a question capable of a "yes" or "no" answer. In reality, the issue is simply the Concise Rule of Law put in the form of a question (e.g., "May an offer be accepted by performance?").

The major problem presented in discerning what is *the* issue in the case is that an opinion usually purports to raise and answer several questions. However, except for rare cases, only one such question is really the issue in the case. Collateral issues not necessary to the resolution of the matter in controversy are handled by the court by language known as *"obiter dictum"* or merely *"dictum."* While dicta may be included later in the brief, it has no place under the issue heading.

To find the issue, the student again asks *who wants what* and then goes on to ask *why did that party succeed or fail in getting it.* Once this is determined, the "why" should be turned into a question.

The complexity of the issues in the cases will vary, but in all cases a single-sentence question should sum up the issue. *In a few cases,* there will be two, or even more rarely, three issues of equal importance to the resolution of the case. Each should be expressed in a single-sentence question.

Since many issues are resolved by a court in coming to a final disposition of a case, the casebook editor will reproduce the portion of the opinion containing the issue or issues most relevant to the area of law under scrutiny. A noted law professor gave this advice: "Close the book; look at the title on the cover." Chances are, if it is Property, the student need not concern himself with whether, for example, the federal government's treatment of the plaintiff's land really raises a federal question sufficient to support jurisdiction on this ground in federal court.

The same rule applies to chapter headings designating sub-areas within the subjects. They tip the student off as to what the text is designed to teach. The cases are arranged in a casebook to show a progression or development of the law, so that the preceding cases may also help.

It is also most important to remember to *read the notes and questions* at the end of a case to determine what the editors wanted the student to have gleaned from it.

HOLDING AND DECISION: This section should succinctly explain the rationale of the court in arriving at its decision. In capsulizing the "reasoning" of the court, it should always include an application of the general rule or rules of law to the specific facts of the case. Hidden justifications come to light in this entry; the reasons for the state of the law, the public policies, the biases and prejudices, those considerations that influence the justices' thinking and, ultimately, the outcome of the case. At the end, there should be a short indication of the disposition or procedural resolution of the case (e.g., "Decision of the trial court for Mr. Smith (P) reversed").

The foregoing format is designed to help you "digest" the reams of case material with which you will be faced in your law school career. Once mastered by practice, it will place at your fingertips the information the authors of your casebooks have sought to impart to you in case-by-case illustration and analysis.

B. BE AS ECONOMICAL AS POSSIBLE IN BRIEFING CASES

Once armed with a format that encourages succinctness, it is as important to be economical with regard to the time spent on the actual reading of the case as it is to be economical in the writing of the brief itself. This does not mean "skimming" a case. Rather, it means reading the case with an "eye" trained to recognize into which "section" of your brief a particular passage or line fits and having a system for quickly and precisely marking the case so that the passages fitting any one particular part of the brief can be easily identified and brought together in a concise and accurate manner when the brief is actually written.

It is of no use to simply repeat everything in the opinion of the court; the student should only record enough information to trigger his or her recollection of what the court said. Nevertheless, an accurate statement of the "law of the case," i.e., the legal principle applied to the facts, is absolutely essential to class preparation and to learning the law under the case method.

To that end, it is important to develop a "shorthand" that you can use to make margin notations. These notations will tell you at a glance in which section of the brief you will be placing that particular passage or portion of the opinion.

Some students prefer to underline all the salient portions of the opinion (with a pencil or colored underliner marker), making marginal notations as they go along. Others prefer the color-coded method of underlining, utilizing different colors of markers to underline the salient portions of the case, each separate color being used to represent a different section of the brief. For example, blue underlining could be used for passages relating to the concise rule of law, yellow for those relating to the issue, and green for those relating to the holding and decision, etc. While it has its advocates, the color-coded method can be confusing and time-consuming (all that time spent on changing colored markers). Furthermore, it can interfere with the continuity and concentration many students deem essential to the reading of a case for maximum comprehension. In the end, however, it is a matter of personal preference and style. Just remember, whatever method you use, underlining must be used sparingly or its value is lost.

For those who take the marginal notation route, an efficient and easy method is to go along underlining the key portions of the case and placing in the margin alongside them the following "markers" to indicate where a particular passage or line "belongs" in the brief you will write:

N (NATURE OF CASE)
CR (CONCISE RULE OF LAW)
I (ISSUE)
HC (HOLDING AND DECISION, relates to the CONCISE RULE OF LAW behind the decision)
HR (HOLDING AND DECISION, gives the RATIONALE or reasoning behind the decision)
HA (HOLDING AND DECISION, APPLIES the general principle(s) of law to the facts of the case to arrive at the decision)

Remember that a particular passage may well contain information necessary to more than one part of your brief, in which case you simply note that in the margin. If you are using the color-coded underlining method instead of margin notation, simply make asterisks or checks in the margin next to the passage in question in the colors that indicate the additional sections of the brief where it might be utilized.

The economy of utilizing "shorthand" in marking cases for briefing can be maintained in the actual brief writing process itself by utilizing "law student shorthand" within the brief. There are many commonly used words and phrases for which abbreviations can be substituted in your briefs (and in your class notes also). You can develop abbreviations that are personal to you and which will save you a lot of time. A reference list of briefing abbreviations will be found elsewhere in this book.

C. USE BOTH THE BRIEFING PROCESS AND THE BRIEF AS A LEARNING TOOL

Now that you have a format and the tools for briefing cases efficiently, the most important thing is to make the time spent in briefing profitable to you and to make the most advantageous use of the briefs you create. Of course, the briefs are invaluable for classroom reference when you are called upon to explain or analyze a particular case. However, they are also useful in reviewing for exams. A quick glance at the fact summary should bring the case to mind, and a rereading of the concise rule of law should enable you to go over the underlying legal concept in your mind, how it was applied in that particular case, and how it might apply in other factual settings.

As to the value to be derived from engaging in the briefing process itself, there is an immediate benefit that arises from being forced to sift through the essential facts and reasoning from the court's opinion and to succinctly express them in your own words in your brief. The process ensures that you understand the case and the point that it illustrates, and that means you will be ready to absorb further analysis and information brought forth in class. It also ensures you will have something to say when called upon in class. The briefing process helps develop a mental agility for getting to the *gist* of a case and for identifying, expounding on, and applying the legal concepts and issues found there. Of most immediate concern, that is the mental process on which you must rely in taking law school examinations. Of more lasting concern, it is also the mental process upon which a lawyer relies in serving his clients and in making his living.

A GLOSSARY OF COMMON LATIN WORDS AND PHRASES ENCOUNTERED IN THE LAW

A FORTIORI: Because one fact exists or has been proven, therefore a second fact that is related to the first fact must also exist.

A PRIORI: From the cause to the effect. A term of logic used to denote that when one generally accepted truth is shown to be a cause, another particular effect must necessarily follow.

AB INITIO: From the beginning; a condition which has existed throughout, as in a marriage which was void ab initio.

ACTUS REUS: The wrongful act; in criminal law, such action sufficient to trigger criminal liability.

AD VALOREM: According to value; an ad valorem tax is imposed upon an item located within the taxing jurisdiction calculated by the value of such item.

AMICUS CURIAE: Friend of the court. Its most common usage takes the form of an amicus curiae brief, filed by a person who is not a party to an action but is nonetheless allowed to offer an argument supporting his legal interests.

ARGUENDO: In arguing. A statement, possibly hypothetical, made for the purpose of argument, is one made arguendo.

BILL QUIA TIMET: A bill to quiet title (establish ownership) to real property.

BONA FIDE: True, honest, or genuine. May refer to a person's legal position based on good faith or lacking notice of fraud (such as a bona fide purchaser for value) or to the authenticity of a particular document (such as a bona fide last will and testament).

CAUSA MORTIS: With approaching death in mind. A gift causa mortis is a gift given by a party who feels certain that death is imminent.

CAVEAT EMPTOR: Let the buyer beware. This maxim is reflected in the rule of law that a buyer purchases at his own risk because it is his responsibility to examine, judge, test, and otherwise inspect what he is buying.

CERTIORARI: A writ of review. Petitions for review of a case by the United States Supreme Court are most often done by means of a writ of certiorari.

CONTRA: On the other hand. Opposite. Contrary to.

CORAM NOBIS: Before us; writs of error directed to the court that originally rendered the judgment.

CORAM VOBIS: Before you; writs of error directed by an appellate court to a lower court to correct a factual error.

CORPUS DELICTI: The body of the crime; the requisite elements of a crime amounting to objective proof that a crime has been committed.

CUM TESTAMENTO ANNEXO, ADMINISTRATOR (ADMINISTRATOR C.T.A.): With will annexed; an administrator c.t.a. settles an estate pursuant to a will in which he is not appointed.

DE BONIS NON, ADMINISTRATOR (ADMINISTRATOR D.B.N.): Of goods not administered; an administrator d.b.n. settles a partially settled estate.

DE FACTO: In fact; in reality; actually. Existing in fact but not officially approved or engendered.

DE JURE: By right; lawful. Describes a condition that is legitimate "as a matter of law," in contrast to the term "de facto," which connotes something existing in fact but not legally sanctioned or authorized. For example, de facto segregation refers to segregation brought about by housing patterns, etc., whereas de jure segregation refers to segregation created by law.

DE MINIMUS: Of minimal importance; insignificant; a trifle; not worth bothering about.

DE NOVO: Anew; a second time; afresh. A trial de novo is a new trial held at the appellate level as if the case originated there and the trial at a lower level had not taken place.

DICTA: Generally used as an abbreviated form of obiter dicta, a term describing those portions of a judicial opinion incidental or not necessary to resolution of the specific question before the court. Such nonessential statements and remarks are not considered to be binding precedent.

DUCES TECUM: Refers to a particular type of writ or subpoena requesting a party or organization to produce certain documents in their possession.

EN BANC: Full bench. Where a court sits with all justices present rather than the usual quorum.

EX PARTE: For one side or one party only. An ex parte proceeding is one undertaken for the benefit of only one party, without notice to, or an appearance by, an adverse party.

EX POST FACTO: After the fact. An ex post facto law is a law that retroactively changes the consequences of a prior act.

EX REL.: Abbreviated form of the term ex relatione, meaning, upon relation or information. When the state brings an action in which it has no interest against an individual at the instigation of one who has a private interest in the matter.

FORUM NON CONVENIENS: Inconvenient forum. Although a court may have jurisdiction over the case, the action should be tried in a more conveniently located court, one to which parties and witnesses may more easily travel, for example.

GUARDIAN AD LITEM: A guardian of an infant as to litigation, appointed to represent the infant and pursue his/her rights.

HABEAS CORPUS: You have the body. The modern writ of habeas corpus is a writ directing that a person (body) being detained (such as a prisoner) be brought before the court so that the legality of his detention can be judicially ascertained.

IN CAMERA: In private, in chambers. When a hearing is held before a judge in his chambers or when all spectators are excluded from the courtroom.

IN FORMA PAUPERIS: In the manner of a pauper. A party who proceeds in forma pauperis because of his poverty is one who is allowed to bring suit without liability for costs.

INFRA: Below, under. A word referring the reader to a later part of a book. (The opposite of supra.)

IN LOCO PARENTIS: In the place of a parent.

IN PARI DELICTO: Equally wrong; a court of equity will not grant requested relief to an applicant who is in pari delicto, or as much at fault in the transactions giving rise to the controversy as is the opponent of the applicant.

IN PARI MATERIA: On like subject matter or upon the same matter. Statutes relating to the same person or things are said to be in pari materia. It is a general rule of statutory construction that such statutes should be construed together, i.e., looked at as if they together constituted one law.

IN PERSONAM: Against the person. Jurisdiction over the person of an individual.

IN RE: In the matter of. Used to designate a proceeding involving an estate or other property.

IN REM: A term that signifies an action against the res, or thing. An action in rem is basically one that is taken directly against property, as distinguished from an action in personam, i.e., against the person.

INTER ALIA: Among other things. Used to show that the whole of a statement, pleading, list, statute, etc., has not been set forth in its entirety.

INTER PARTES: Between the parties. May refer to contracts, conveyances or other transactions having legal significance.

INTER VIVOS: Between the living. An inter vivos gift is a gift made by a living grantor, as distinguished from bequests contained in a will, which pass upon the death of the testator.

IPSO FACTO: By the mere fact itself.

JUS: Law or the entire body of law.

LEX LOCI: The law of the place; the notion that the rights of parties to a legal proceeding are governed by the law of the place where those rights arose.

MALUM IN SE: Evil or wrong in and of itself; inherently wrong. This term describes an act that is wrong by its very nature, as opposed to one which would not be wrong but for the fact that there is a specific legal prohibition against it (malum prohibitum).

MALUM PROHIBITUM: Wrong because prohibited, but not inherently evil. Used to describe something that is wrong because it is expressly forbidden by law but that is not in and of itself evil, e.g., speeding.

MANDAMUS: We command. A writ directing an official to take a certain action.

MENS REA: A guilty mind; a criminal intent. A term used to signify the mental state that accompanies a crime or other prohibited act. Some crimes require only a general mens rea (general intent to do the prohibited act), but others, like assault with intent to murder, require the existence of a specific mens rea.

MODUS OPERANDI: Method of operating; generally refers to the manner or style of a criminal in committing crimes, admissible in appropriate cases as evidence of the identity of a defendant.

NEXUS: A connection to.

NISI PRIUS: A court of first impression. A nisi prius court is one where issues of fact are tried before a judge or jury.

N.O.V. (NON OBSTANTE VEREDICTO): Notwithstanding the verdict. A judgment n.o.v. is a judgment given in favor of one party despite the fact that a verdict was returned in favor of the other party, the justification being that the verdict either had no reasonable support in fact or was contrary to law.

NUNC PRO TUNC: Now for then. This phrase refers to actions that may be taken and will then have full retroactive effect.

PENDENTE LITE: Pending the suit; pending litigation underway.

PER CAPITA: By head; beneficiaries of an estate, if they take in equal shares, take per capita.

PER CURIAM: By the court; signifies an opinion ostensibly written "by the whole court" and with no identified author.

PER SE: By itself, in itself; inherently.

PER STIRPES: By representation. Used primarily in the law of wills to describe the method of distribution where a person, generally because of death, is unable to take that which is left to him by the will of another, and therefore his heirs divide such property between them rather than take under the will individually.

PRIMA FACIE: On its face, at first sight. A prima facie case is one that is sufficient on its face, meaning that the evidence supporting it is adequate to establish the case until contradicted or overcome by other evidence.

PRO TANTO: For so much; as far as it goes. Often used in eminent domain cases when a property owner receives partial payment for his land without prejudice to his right to bring suit for the full amount he claims his land to be worth.

QUANTUM MERUIT: As much as he deserves. Refers to recovery based on the doctrine of unjust enrichment in those cases in which a party has rendered valuable services or furnished materials that were accepted and enjoyed by another under circumstances that would reasonably notify the recipient that the rendering party expected to be paid. In essence, the law implies a contract to pay the reasonable value of the services or materials furnished.

QUASI: Almost like; as if; nearly. This term is essentially used to signify that one subject or thing is almost analogous to another but that material differences between them do exist. For example, a quasi-criminal proceeding is one that is not strictly criminal but shares enough of the same characteristics to require some of the same safeguards (e.g., procedural due process must be followed in a parol hearing).

QUID PRO QUO: Something for something. In contract law, the consideration, something of value, passed between the parties to render the contract binding.

RES GESTAE: Things done; in evidence law, this principle justifies the admission of a statement that would otherwise be hearsay when it is made so closely to the event in question as to be said to be a part of it, or with such spontaneity as not to have the possibility of falsehood.

RES IPSA LOQUITUR: The thing speaks for itself. This doctrine gives rise to a rebuttable presumption of negligence when the instrumentality causing the injury was within the exclusive control of the defendant, and the injury was one that does not normally occur unless a person has been negligent.

RES JUDICATA: A matter adjudged. Doctrine which provides that once a court of competent jurisdiction has rendered a final judgment or decree on the merits, that judgment or decree is conclusive upon the parties to the case and prevents them from engaging in any other litigation on the points and issues determined therein.

RESPONDEAT SUPERIOR: Let the master reply. This doctrine holds the master liable for the wrongful acts of his servant (or the principal for his agent) in those cases in which the servant (or agent) was acting within the scope of his authority at the time of the injury.

STARE DECISIS: To stand by or adhere to that which has been decided. The common law doctrine of stare decisis attempts to give security and certainty to the law by following the policy that once a principle of law as applicable to a certain set of facts has been set forth in a decision, it forms a precedent which will subsequently be followed, even though a different decision might be made were it the first time the question had arisen. Of course, stare decisis is not an inviolable principle and is departed from in instances where there is good cause (e.g., considerations of public policy led the Supreme Court to disregard prior decisions sanctioning segregation).

SUPRA: Above. A word referring a reader to an earlier part of a book.

ULTRA VIRES: Beyond the power. This phrase is most commonly used to refer to actions taken by a corporation that are beyond the power or legal authority of the corporation.

ADDENDUM OF FRENCH DERIVATIVES

IN PAIS: Not pursuant to legal proceedings.

CHATTEL: Tangible personal property.

CY PRES: Doctrine permitting courts to apply trust funds to purposes not expressed in the trust but necessary to carry out the settlor's intent.

PER AUTRE VIE: For another's life; in property law, an estate may be granted that will terminate upon the death of someone other than the grantee.

PROFIT A PRENDRE: A license to remove minerals or other produce from land.

VOIR DIRE: Process of questioning jurors as to their predispositions about the case or parties to a proceeding in order to identify those jurors displaying bias or prejudice.

NOTES

TABLE OF CASES

NOTES

TABLE OF CASES (Continued)

SELLERS v. AMERICAN BROADCASTING CO.

668 F.2d 1207 (11th Cir. 1982).

NATURE OF CASE: Appeal of summary judgment dismissing action for copyright infringement.

FACT SUMMARY: Sellers (P) sued for ABC's (D) broadcast of a theory regarding a celebrity's death which Sellers (P) claimed was similar to a scenario he had related to it in general terms.

CONCISE RULE OF LAW: Broad, general statements may not form the basis of a copyright infringement action.

FACTS: Sellers (P), an investigative reporter, contacted Rivera (D), another reporter with connections to the American Broadcasting Co. (D), that he had a "story" on the death of recording star Elvis Presley. Rivera (D), ABC (D), and Sellers (P) contracted with each other that the latter would provide the others with the story. The story turned out to be broad, general allegations about prescription drug irregularities. Rivera (D) and ABC (D) declined to feature the story, due to lack of corroboration. About a year later, ABC (D) broadcast a program regarding Presley, in which the possibility of prescription drug interaction was featured. Sellers (P) sued for breach of contract and copyright infringement. The district court granted summary judgment dismissing the suit, and Sellers (P) appealed.

ISSUE: May broad, general statements form the basis of a copyright infringement action?

HOLDING AND DECISION: (Johnson, J.) No. Broad, general statements may not form the basis of a copyright infringement action. A copyright and/or misappropriation action will be allowed only when the allegedly copyrighted material is concrete. Broad, general matters are not subject to copyright or misappropriation. Here, Sellers (P) propounded the idea that Presley died due to problems with prescription drugs, but his allegations were not specific; in fact, it appears that their focus was different from that used in ABC's (D) program. For that reason, no misappropriation or infringement occurred. Affirmed.

EDITOR'S ANALYSIS: New York law in this instance had three elements for a misappropriation action. The misappropriated idea had to be novel, it had to be concrete, and it had to be used by the defendant. While the court here only focused on the second element, it seems that it could have concluded that the third element was not met either.

NOTES:

LUEDDECKE v. CHEVROLET MOTOR CO.

70 F.2d 345 (8th Cir. 1934).

NATURE OF CASE: Appeal of demurrer dismissing action for damages for breach of contract.

FACT SUMMARY: Lueddecke (P) claimed that he was entitled compensation for Chevrolet's (D) incorporation into its auto design several unsolicited suggestions he had made.

CONCISE RULE OF LAW: A party is not legally liable for incorporating into its product generalized suggestions regarding the product.

FACTS: Lueddecke (P) forwarded an unsolicited letter to Chevrolet Motor Co. (D), informing it of a design problem in a line of its autos and offering to provide suggestions to ameliorate the problem. When Chevrolet (D) responded that it would only consider specific suggestions, Lueddecke (P) informed it that the autos tended to sag to the left side, and he suggested certain common-sense solutions such as repositioning certain components. Chevrolet eventually alleviated the problem, doing several things Lueddecke (P) had suggested. When Chevrolet (D) refused to compensate Lueddecke (P), he sued for breach of implied contract. The district court sustained Chevrolet's (D) demurrer, and Lueddecke (P) appealed.

ISSUE: Is a party legally liable for incorporating into its product generalized suggestions made regarding the product?

HOLDING AND DECISION: (Woodrough, J.) No. A party is not legally liable for incorporating into its product generalized suggestions made regarding its product. For an idea to rise to the level of a property right, it must be novel and useful. While an idea need not necessarily be copyrighted or patented to be novel, it does need to be demonstrably new. Such an idea also needs to be specific. A common-sense idea relating to a product in a generalized way is not novel. Here, the perceived problem with the autos was a left-side tilt. Lueddecke's (P) proffered cure was the logical solution of redistributing weight, an idea which cannot be called novel. For this reason, Lueddecke (P) could not obtain a proprietary interest in the idea sufficient to form the basis of an implied contract. Affirmed.

EDITOR'S ANALYSIS: As the present case illustrates, the road is not easy for one originating ideas only. Generally speaking, copyright and patent law protects those who originate and develop. An originator only is most likely to end up without recourse, as Lueddecke (P) discovered.

NOTES:

DOWNEY v. GENERAL FOODS CORP.

N.Y. Ct. App., 31 N.Y.2d 56 (1972).

NATURE OF CASE: Consideration of certified issue of law in an action for damages for idea misappropriation.

FACT SUMMARY: General Foods Corp. (D) independently developed a marketing idea which was suggested to it by Downey (P).

CONCISE RULE OF LAW: A party does not misappropriate another's idea if it develops the idea independently.

FACTS: General Foods Corp. (D) manufactured the gelatin product "Jell-O." Downey (P), an individual not affiliated with the company, mailed in a suggestion that it be marketed for children under a variation of the word "wiggle." General Foods (D) responded that it was not interested. Several months later, however, General Foods (D) marketed a children's gelatin product called "Mr. Wiggle." Downey (P) sued for misappropriation. Uncontroverted evidence showed that General Foods' (D) marketing division had independently formulated the label. Both sides moved for summary judgment. The trial court denied the motions, and the appellate division affirmed. The state court of appeals accepted a certified issue of law.

ISSUE: Does a party misappropriate another's idea if it develops the idea independently?

HOLDING AND DECISION: (Fuld, C.J.) No. A party does not misappropriate another's idea if it develops the idea independently. In order for an idea to constitute intellectual property, it must be novel and original. When two parties independently develop a certain idea, the idea itself is not novel or original, and neither party has a proprietary interest therein. Here, evidence shows that both Downey (P) and General Foods (D) independently developed the "Mr. Wiggle" idea, and therefore Downey (P) had no proprietary right in General Foods' (D) use of it. Remanded with directions to enter judgment in favor of General Foods (D).

EDITOR'S ANALYSIS: Generally speaking, the concept of idea as property has not fared well in the courts. If a plaintiff cannot fit his cause of action into the pigeonhole of patent or trade secret, he faces a tough road. California briefly provided an exception to this rule, but the practice did not last long even in that traditionally plaintiff-hospitable state.

NOTES:

ARONSON v. QUICK POINT PENCIL CO.

440 U.S. 257 (1979).

NATURE OF CASE: Review of declaratory judgment voiding a marketing contract.

FACT SUMMARY: Quick Point Pencil (P) sought to escape a contract to pay royalties to Aronson (D) on a product the latter invented but was unable to patent.

CONCISE RULE OF LAW: Failure to obtain a patent by an inventor will not preclude enforcement of a contract paying royalties on the invention to the inventor.

FACTS: Aronson (D) designed a keyholder. She applied for a patent. At the same time she contracted with Quick Point Pencil Co. (P) for the latter to manufacture and market the product. Aronson (D) was to receive a 2½% royalty on each unit sold, to be increased to 5% if a patent was issued. The product sold well, selling over seven million units the first three years. However, the patent office rejected the application, and copycat products began to appear, manufactured by concerns not obligated to pay monies to Aronson (D). Quick Point (P) commenced a federal suit seeking a declaration that the contract was void, being preempted by federal patent law. The district court granted summary judgment dismissing the action, but the court of appeals reversed. The Supreme Court granted certiorari.

ISSUE: Will failure to obtain a patent by an inventor preclude enforcement of a contract paying royalties on the invention to the inventor?

HOLDING AND DECISION: (Burger, C.J.) No. Failure to obtain a patent by an inventor will not preclude enforcement of a contract paying royalties on the invention to the inventor. Federal patent law does not expressly preempt state laws regarding contracts covering inventions. This being the case, patent law may only be held to preempt such state laws if enforcement of such laws is antithetical to the purposes of patent law. The purposes of such law are to encourage invention, promote disclosure of inventions, and promote further innovation. State laws protecting contractual rights in nonpatentable inventions do not conflict with these goals. They provide some, albeit lesser, encouragement of invention. Further, enforcement of such a contract in no way discourages disclosure of inventions. Finally, no negative effect on further innovation can be discerned by this Court. In view of these considerations, and the lack of any precedent to the contrary, the only proper conclusion is that federal patent law does not preempt state law covering royalties on inventions. Reversed.

CONCURRENCE: (Blackmun, J.) A royalty agreement on a patent product extending beyond the maximum term of a patent would be suspect.

EDITOR'S ANALYSIS: This case may be seen as providing less of a concrete rule and more of a guideline. The overriding principle to be discerned is that state idea protection laws may not conflict with federal patent law. Justice Blackmun provided an example of what law that would, in his opinion, so conflict. Analysis of such laws would have to be on a case-by-case basis.

NOTES:

WILLIAM R. WARNER & CO. v. ELI LILLY & CO.

265 U.S. 526 (1924).

NATURE OF CASE: Review of order enjoining drug manufacture.

FACT SUMMARY: William R. Warner & Co. (D) attempted to market a drug as a substitute for an identical drug manufactured by Eli Lilly & Co. (P).

CONCISE RULE OF LAW: A manufacturer may not pass off its product as the product of another.

FACTS: Eli Lilly & Co. (P) manufactured a product called Coco-Quinine, in which quinine was suspended in a chocolate preparation to make it palatable. Subsequent to this, William R. Warner & Co. (P) began to market an identical product called Quin-Coco. In its marketing campaign, Warner (D) encouraged druggists to substitute Quin-Coco in prescriptions calling for Coco-Quinine, as it was identical in composition and lesser in price. Lilly (P) filled an action to enjoin this practice, contending that it constituted unfair competition. The court of appeals, finding unfair competition, enjoined the manufacture of Quin-Coco. Warner (D) petitioned for certiorari to the Supreme Court.

ISSUE: May a manufacturer pass off its product as the product of another?

HOLDING AND DECISION: (Sutherland, J.) No. A manufacturer may not pass off its product as the product of another. A party is fully entitled to manufacture a product identical to any other nonpatented product. However, that party may not attempt to convince the buying public that its product is the same as the original. It may compare its product favorably to the original, but it must keep the products distinct. In this instance, Warner (D) actively attempted to induce druggists to substitute Quin-Coco for Coco-Quinine, which would result in a fraud upon the buying public. This constituted unfair competition, not manufacture of the product itself. In light of these considerations, the injunction against the manufacture of Quin-Coco was too broad. Rather, the appropriate remedy is an injunction prohibiting Warner's (D) palming off Quin-Coco as Coco-Quinine. Reversed and remanded.

EDITOR'S ANALYSIS: The names Quin-Coco and Coco-Quinine were obviously similar. However, no cause of action existed for trademark infringement. Both names were descriptive of the product contents. A name which is a mere description cannot be trademarked so as to prevent other items fitting the description from also incorporating descriptive terms.

NOTES:

GALT HOUSE, INC. v. HOME SUPPLY CO.

Ky. Ct. App., 483 S.W.2d 107, 174 U.S.P.Q. 268 (1972).

NATURE OF CASE: Appeal of denial of injunction against use of trade name.

FACT SUMMARY: Galt House, Inc. (P), which had never done business, sought to enjoin Home Supply Co. (D) from operating an establishment called "The Galt House."

CONCISE RULE OF LAW: A corporation which has not done business may not prevent others from employing a DBA identical to that corporation's name.

FACTS: A succession of hotels in Louisville, Kentucky, spanning nearly a century, were called "The Galt House." The last Galt House closed its doors in 1920. In 1964, Galt House, Inc. (P) was incorporated. Its incorporator wished to open a hotel of that name, but the project never materialized. In 1970, Home Supply Co. (D) opened a large hotel bearing the name. Galt House, Inc. (P) filed a suit seeking to enjoin the use of the name. The trial court declined to issue the injunction, and Galt House, Inc. (P) appealed.

ISSUE: May a corporation which has not done business prevent others from employing a DBA identical to that corporation's name?

HOLDING AND DECISION: (Reed, J.) No. A corporation which has not done business may not prevent others from employing a DBA identical to that corporation's name. Such a corporation certainly cannot use unfair competition as a basis for such action, since unfair competition involves the appropriation of another's goodwill. One not having done business has no goodwill. A corporation not having done business, to be able to prohibit others from using its name, would have to rely on the principle that the mere incorporation of a name gives it a proprietary interest therein. There is no precedent for such a contention, and this court sees no reason to adopt it. Incorporation in a certain name should not confer a perpetual monopoly on the name. Since Galt House, Inc.'s (P) only claim to its name is the act of incorporation, it cannot claim a right to exclusive use of the name. Affirmed.

EDITOR'S ANALYSIS: The linchpin of unfair competition is confusion. Unfair competition exists when the unfair competitor's marketing practices are likely to cause confusion in the minds of the purchasing public as to whose product it is purchasing. Where there is no prior product with which to be confused, as was the case here, there can be no such confusion.

NOTES:

THE SAMPLE, INC. v. PORRATH
N.Y. App. Div., 41 A.D.2d 118 (1973).

NATURE OF CASE: Appeal of injunction prohibiting opening of retail establishment.

FACT SUMMARY: The Porraths (D) objected to the entry of The Sample, Inc.'s (P) similarly-named shop into their market area, even though The Sample, Inc.'s (P) stores were better known to the local public.

CONCISE RULE OF LAW: A local business cannot enjoin anther business from using the same name in its market if the local public is more familiar with the name of the nonlocal business.

FACTS: The Sample, Inc. (P) operated a series of retail outlets in New York state. Each store was called "The Sample." The Porraths (D) operated two stores in the Niagara area called "The Sample Shop." When The Sample, Inc. (P) began showing an interest in opening an outlet in Niagara, the Porraths (D) objected. The Sample, Inc. (P) filed an action seeking a declaration that it could enter the Niagara market. The Porraths (D) cross-claimed for an injunction prohibiting such entry. A consumer survey showed a majority of Niagara residents identified the stores operated by The Sample (P), not those of the Porraths (D). The trial court enjoined The Sample, Inc. (P) from entering the Niagara market, and The Sample, Inc. (P) appealed.

ISSUE: Can a local business enjoin another business from using the same name in its market if the local public is more familiar with the name of the nonlocal business?

HOLDING AND DECISION: (Goldman, J.) No. A local business cannot enjoin another business from using the same name in its market if the local public is more familiar with the name of the nonlocal business. A party has the right to enjoin another's use of a commercial name only if such use is unfair. That unfairness exists when the party seeking the injunction has expended time and effort to familiarize the public with its name and product, and the offending party seeks to exploit that effort. When the public has not in fact come to associate a certain product or service with a name, the use of it by another is perfectly legitimate. Here, evidence showed that, despite the local character of the Porrath's (D) operations and the nonlocal character of those of The Sample, Inc. (P), the Niagara public still identified the term "Sample" with The Sample (P), not the Sample Shop. This being so, the Porraths (D) were not entitled to enjoin The Sample, Inc. (P) from employing the name. Reversed.

EDITOR'S ANALYSIS: The association of a product or service to a commercial name is called a "secondary meaning." At one time, the be-all and end-all of an unfair competition cause of action was whether a product had acquired a secondary meaning. In recent times, courts have tended to use terms such as "fair" and "unfair" rather than look to the concept of secondary meanings.

NOTES:

MEAD DATA CENTRAL, INC. v. TOYOTA MOTOR SALES, U.S.A., INC

875 F.2d 1026 (2d Cir. 1989).

NATURE OF CASE: Appeal of injunction prohibiting the promulgation of a product name.

FACT SUMMARY: Mead Data (P) and Toyota (D) put out two products which, although very similar in name, were highly unlikely to be linked in the public mind.

CONCISE RULE OF LAW: A junior product manufacturer does not dilute the market of a senior manufacturer if no likelihood exists of a linkage between the two products in the public mind.

FACTS: Mead Data Central, Inc. (P) provided a data retrieval service used almost exclusively by lawyers and accountants, called "Lexis." Subsequent to this, Toyota Motor Sales, U.S.A., Inc. (D) announced a plan to manufacture and market, through a subsidiary, an automobile called "Lexus." Mead (P) objected that this infringed on their interest in the name "Lexis," but Toyota (D) went ahead with the product line. Mead Data (P) filed an action seeking to enjoin use of the name. Evidence showed that the name "Lexis" was virtually unknown outside the legal and accounting communities. The district court found Toyota (D) in violation of New York's antidilution statute and enjoined use of the name. Toyota (D) appealed.

ISSUE: Does a junior product manufacturer dilute the market of a senior manufacturer if no likelihood exists of linkage between the two products in the public mind?

HOLDING AND DECISION: (Van Graafeiland, J.) No. A junior product manufacturer does not dilute the market of a senior manufacturer if no likelihood exists of linkage between the two products in the public mind. New York's antidilution statute does not require that a junior product or service directly compete with the market of the senior product or service; all that is required is the unauthorized use of a distinctive quality of a mark or trade name. This is done to protect the maker of an established product service from being exploited by the use of its name. However, for dilution to occur, the mark or name in question must in fact be distinctive. Where the name is one of common usage or does not have a distinctive quality, dilution cannot occur. Here, the term "Lexis" incorporates the prefix "lex," a common prefix donating "word." Further, evidence shows that the public's recognition of the term "Lexis" is virtually nil. This being so, dilution cannot occur. Reversed.

EDITOR'S ANALYSIS: "Dilution" is a variation of unfair competition. While the requirements of the two vary from state to state, the former can generally be distinguished from the latter by a lack of requirement of direct competition. A junior product may dilute if it attempts to use the notoriety of another's name, even if it does not actually compete in its market.

NOTES:

BOARD OF TRADE OF CITY OF CHICAGO v. DOW JONES & CO.

Ill. Sup. Ct., 98 Ill. 2d 109 (1983).

NATURE OF CASE: Appeal of order enjoining use of a stock futures index.

FACT SUMMARY: Dow Jones & Co. (D) objected to the use of its index in a financial service it did not offer.

CONCISE RULE OF LAW: A party's product or service may be misappropriated even if the appropriating party offers a product unlike any offered by the other party.

FACTS: The Board of Trade of the City of Chicago (P) was the largest commodities exchange market in the United States. Member brokerages traded commodities futures contracts there much in the same manner that stock is traded in a stock exchange. Dow Jones & Co. (D) offered a variety of financial services, including the most closely-watched stock index in the country, the Dow Jones 30 Industrials average. In 1982 the practice of trading in stock market futures contracts, in which stock index futures were traded much in the manner of commodities futures, was instituted. As with commodities futures, success at this particular investment depended upon which direction the market went, in this case the market being either individual stocks or mutual funds. The index adopted by the Board (P) was based on the same companies as those utilized by Dow Jones (D). Even though the Board (P) disclaimed any relation with Dow Jones (D), its company selection had the practical result of the indexes being the same. Anticipating Dow Jones' (D) reaction, the Board (P) filed an action seeking a declaration that its practice was permissible. Dow Jones (D) cross-claimed for an injunction against the use of the index. The trial court entered judgment in favor of the Board (P) , but the appellate court reversed, and enjoined the use of the index. The Board (P) appealed.

ISSUE: May a party's product or service be misappropriated even if the appropriating party offers a product unlike any offered by the other party?

HOLDING AND DECISION: (Goldenhersh, J.) Yes. A party's product or service may be misappropriated even if the appropriating party offers a product unlike any offered by the other party. This particular issue presents a conflict of philosophies regarding the concept of misappropriation. The Board (P) argues that since the parties are not in competition with each other, use of Dow Jones' (D) index results in no loss to Dow Jones (D). The counterargument to this, as stated by Dow (D), is that misappropriation as a concept must be flexible so that "enterprising pirates" cannot avoid application of the doctrine. Framing these arguments are the larger competing principles that on the one hand an innovative party deserves the fruits of its labor, while on the other hand, allowing imitation pushes all parties to innovate further. When all is said and done, the overriding concern in any case is whether social utility is better served by allowing or prohibiting appropriation. Whether the parties occupy the same market is a consideration, but only one of several. Here, Dow Jones (D) has expended much time, energy, and money to achieve its highly respected status. In the context of stock market futures, any type of index can be used; giving Dow Jones (D) a monopoly on its 30 industrials hardly stifles the stock market futures market. In fact, doing so may encourage innovation by forcing experimentation. In light of these considerations, the better decision is that the Board (P) be prohibited from using Dow Jones' (D) index. Affirmed.

EDITOR'S ANALYSIS: The first major enunciation of misappropriation as a theory came in International News Service v. Associated Press, 248 U.S. 215 (1918). There, International was prohibited from running stories it appropriated from Associated. The main difference between that case and the present one was that there the markets were identical.

NOTES:

DAVID B. FINDLAY, INC. v. FINDLAY

N.Y. Ct. App., 18 N.Y.2d 12 (1966).

NATURE OF CASE: Appeal of injunction prohibiting the use of trade name.

FACT SUMMARY: Findlay (D) was enjoined from using his name on the basis that such use could cause confusion with the similarly-named establishment located next to his.

CONCISE RULE OF LAW: An individual may be enjoined from using his own name in a business if such use would lead to confusion with another business.

FACTS: David (P) and Wally (D) Findlay, brothers, both operated art galleries specializing in impressionist and post-impressionist paintings. David (P) operated a gallery in Manhattan named "Findlay Galleries." Wally (D) had a gallery in Chicago. At one point Wally (D) opened up a gallery in Manhattan, immediately adjacent to David's (P) establishment, and called it "Wally Findlay Galleries." David (P) brought an action seeking to enjoin the use by Wally (D) of the name "Findlay" in his gallery. The trial court issued such an injunction. The appellate division affirmed. Wally (D) appealed to the state high court, contending that he had an absolute right to use his name in his business.

ISSUE: May an individual be enjoined from using his own name in a business if such use would lead to confusion with another business?

HOLDING AND DECISION: (Keating, J.) Yes. An individual may be enjoined from using his own name in a business if such use would lead to confusion with another business. It is true that an individual has a property interest in his own name. However, no unlimited "sacred right" to use one's name in a business exists. A person's name, like any other name, may not be used to appropriate the goodwill of another business by causing confusion in the mind of the buying public. Here, the trial court found that, since both galleries were adjacent to each other and specialized in the same type of art, the chance for confusion was great. It issued a narrowly-framed injunction to remedy this chance of confusion. This was an entirely appropriate action on the part of the trial court and should not be reversed. Affirmed.

EDITOR'S ANALYSIS: Courts have always been fairly lenient about letting an individual use his name in a trade or business. One challenging such a use will generally have to make out a clear case of unfair competition. However, when such a showing is made, injunctive relief is appropriate.

NOTES:

SULLIVAN v. ED SULLIVAN RADIO & T.V., INC.

N.Y. App. Div., 1 A.D.2d 609 (1956).

NATURE OF CASE: Appeal of denial of injunction against use of trade name.

FACT SUMMARY: Sullivan (P) a prominent radio and television personality, objected to use of the name "Ed" rather than "Edward" or some other variant by Ed Sullivan Radio & T.V., Inc. (D), which operated a television and radio repair business.

CONCISE RULE OF LAW: Use of a particular variant of one's own name may be prohibited.

FACTS: Ed Sullivan (P) was a prominent radio and television personality. Edward J. Sullivan (D) formed a corporation named "Ed Sullivan Radio & T.V., Inc." (D), through which he operated a television and radio repair business. Sullivan (P) brought an action seeking to enjoin the use of the "Ed" variant of the name "Edward," contending that such use would lead to confusion in the minds of the public. The trial court denied the injunction, and Sullivan (P) appealed.

ISSUE: May use of a particular variant of one's own name be prohibited?

HOLDING AND DECISION: (Cox, J.) Yes. Use of a particular variant of one's own name may be prohibited. Although courts usually will not interfere with the right of a person to use his own name in a business, the present trend of the law is to enjoin the use even of a family name where such use tends to induce confusion in the public mind. This is equally true with respect to various possible permutations of a name. Here, Sullivan (P) is extremely well-known in the television industry. While a television-repair business does not directly compete with him, use of his name by anyone connected with television might create an inference in the public mind of some connection. This would constitute unfair competition and should be enjoined. Reversed.

EDITOR'S ANALYSIS: The analysis in unfair competition involving personal names is in fact no different than any trade name. Any such use tending to create such confusion is enjoinable. As in any such case, whether such confusion exists must be analyzed in light of factors such as the notoriety of the senior name and the similarity of the junior name.

NOTES:

CRESCENT TOOL CO. v. KILBORN & BISHOP CO.

247 F. 299 (2nd. Cir. 1917).

NATURE OF CASE: Appeal of injunction against product manufacture and sales.

NOTES:

FACT SUMMARY: Kilborn & Bishop (D) manufactured wrenches possessing the same basic shape and function as wrenches manufactured by Crescent Tool Co. (P).

CONCISE RULE OF LAW: A product may be marketed having the same shape and function as a senior product if the public is not likely to believe when purchasing the junior product that it is purchasing the senior product.

FACTS: In 1908, Crescent Tool Co. (P) began marketing an adjustable wrench. In 1910, Kilborn & Bishop Co. (D) began marketing its own adjustable wrench. This wrench was similar in shape and function to the wrench manufactured by Crescent (P), but lacked the name "Crescent Tool Co." stamped on Crescent's (P) product and instead had its own mark. The wrench came in a package dissimilar to that provided by Crescent (P), and Kilborn (D) did not market the wrench as a Crescent (P) wrench. Crescent (P) brought an action seeking to enjoin the manufacture and sale of the Kilborn (D) wrench. The district court entered such an order, and Kilborn (D) appealed.

ISSUE: May a product be marketed having the same shape and function as a senior product if the public is not likely to believe that when purchasing the junior product that it is purchasing the senior product?

HOLDING AND DECISION: (Hand, J.) Yes. A product may be marketed having the same shape and function as a senior product if the public is not likely to believe when purchasing the junior product that it is purchasing the senior product. A necessary condition for a product manufacturer to enjoin the manufacture of a similar product is proof that the public perceives the product in question to be made by the senior manufacturer, and a belief in the public mind that when it buys a product that it is buying the product of that manufacturer and no one else. That another's product may be similar in style and function will not give rise to unfair competition if the public realizes when it is buying the junior product that the junior product is not the senior manufacturer's product. Here, no evidence existed tending to prove that the public was confused in this manner, so Kilborn's (D) marketing was completely legitimate. Reversed.

EDITOR'S ANALYSIS: Cases such as this turn on the issue of whether the junior product can fairly be referred to as a "copycat" product. A senior manufacturer not having a patent has no claim on a product's style or function, and any other person may sell a product having the same shape or use. Impropriety only exists when a junior manufacturer copies nonfunctional elements of a senior product tending to give it a distinctive appearance.

SEARS, ROEBUCK & CO. v. STIFFEL CO.

376 U.S. 225, 140 U.S.P.Q. 524 (1964).

NATURE OF CASE: Action seeking damages for unfair competition.

FACT SUMMARY: Although Stiffel (P) had obtained design and mechanical patents on a "pole lamp" it placed on the market, Sears (D) thereafter began to sell its own version at a much cheaper price.

CONCISE RULE OF LAW: A state's unfair competition law cannot impose liability for or prohibit the copying of an article which is unprotectable under either the federal patent or copyright laws.

FACTS: Having designed a pole lamp that it marketed, Stiffel (P) obtained both design and mechanical patents thereon. In a short time, Sears (D) came out with the same lamp, but it sold at a much cheaper price. As a result, Stiffel (P) brought an action seeking damages for unfair competition, but the court held that the patents Stiffel (P) had secured were invalid for want of invention. It nonetheless recognized that the lamps were substantially identical and, noting that customers might be confused, the court held that Sears (D) had engaged in unfair competition by marketing the confusingly similar lamps. From that decision, Sears (D) appealed, the court of appeals affirmed, and the Supreme Court granted certiorari.

ISSUE: If a particular article is one which neither the federal patent or copyright laws protect, can a state's unfair competition law impose liability for or prohibit the copying the article?

HOLDING AND DECISION: (Black, J.) No. Just as a state can not directly encroach upon federal patent or copyright law, it may not use its own laws on unfair competition or any other subject to protect an article which is left unprotected under the aforementioned federal laws. These federal systems of protection have occupied the field, and state law in those areas is preempted by the applicable federal scheme. Thus, where, as in this case, a state's unfair competition law clashes with the objectives of federal patent or copyright law, in providing a uniform system of protection while also preserving free competition where it is deemed appropriate, it must yield under the doctrine of preemption. Since Stiffel (P) was unable to obtain protection under the federal copyright or patent laws, its article was among those the federal scheme desired to leave unprotected, and the state cannot enter into the picture and extend protection. Reversed.

EDITOR'S ANALYSIS: The preemption doctrine, on which this case was decided, flows from the Supremacy Clause in Article IV of the Constitution, which makes federally enacted laws the supreme law of the land. The result is that when Congress passes laws that "occupy" a particular field, that action serves to "preempt" states from taking individual action in that area. It is an important concept in dealing with patents and copyrights, for a national system of protection could easily be thwarted and would be all but useless were inventors and authors uncertain whether their federal rights were effectively altered depending upon which state they were in. This type of uncertainty would have a damaging effect on the generation of new ideas and new products, which really depends on a nationwide standard of protection.

NOTES:

COMPCO CORP. v. DAY-BRITE LIGHTING, INC.

376 U.S. 234, 140 U.S.P.Q. 531 (1964).

NATURE OF CASE: Appeal from affirmation of a decision enjoining the sale of certain articles as "unfair competition."

FACT SUMMARY: Compco (D) began manufacturing fluorescent lighting fixtures substantially identical to those upon which Day-Brite (P) had secured a design patent that turned out to be invalid.

CONCISE RULE OF LAW: A state cannot use its unfair competition laws to prohibit or give relief for copying an article which is unpatentable under federal law and therefore in the public domain.

FACTS: When Day-Brite (P) sued to enjoin Compco (D) from producing a fluorescent lighting fixture almost identical to one on which it had secured a design patent, but not a mechanical patent, the court found that the design patent was invalid. However, it still issued the injunction, and the appellate court affirmed that decision. The basis thereof was the contention that the similarity of the fixtures would cause a confusion as to source which would be violative of the state unfair competition law. Compco (D), which clearly labeled both the fixtures and the containers in which they were shipped, appealed that decision. It was apparent that Compco (D) does not sell through manufacturer's representatives handling competing lines, including those of Day-Brite (P), but that once the fixtures are in place it is hard to tell them apart.

ISSUE: Can a state forbid one from copying an article on the basis that such would violate state unfair competition laws by causing confusion as to source if said article is not protected by the federal laws on patents and copyrights?

HOLDING AND DECISION: (Black, J.) No. Where an article is left unprotected, and therefore in the public domain, under federal patent and copyrights laws, a state cannot prevent the copying of such an article on the basis that its unfair competition law would be violated due to the probability of confusion as to source. To allow such an indirect assault on federal patent law would be to sanction a state's attempt to give a kind of protection which clashes with the objectives of those federal laws; one of those objectives is to allow free access to copy whatever the federal laws leave in the public domain. As we have stated in other cases, a state can act to impose liability for "palming off" or require labeling to prevent confusion as to source, but it cannot impose liability for or prohibit the actual acts of copying and selling unpatentable articles. The same holds true for an unpatentable design, whether or not it is a design which identifies its maker to the trade. Of course, liability for failure to label or identify such copied goods cannot occur validly unless there is a valid state statute or decisional law requiring the copier to label or take other precautions to prevent confusion of customers as to the source of the goods. Here, the judgment below resulting in an injunction and an accounting for damages was based on the mere act of copying and not on such labeling laws. Therefore, that decision must be reversed.

CONCURRENCE: (Harlan, J.) If copying is found to have been undertaken with the dominant purpose and effect of palming off one's goods as those of another, the state may impose reasonable restrictions on future copying.

EDITOR'S ANALYSIS: The doctrine of preemption has become extremely important in the past few years as states have tried to strengthen their own laws regarding unfair competition, trade secrets, etc., to deal with the increasing problem of copiers siphoning off profits from industries which are particularly vulnerable. In response to a particular problem in the record industry, the Court backed off from the seemingly stringent position taken herein and allowed California to protect its record industry from pirating via state laws (see the next case, Goldstein).

NOTES:

FOREST LABORATORIES, INC. v. FORMULATIONS, INC.

299 F.Supp. 202 (D. Wis. 1969).

NOTES:

NATURE OF CASE: Action for damages and injunctive relief for improper use of trade secrets.

FACT SUMMARY: Pillsbury (D) contended that no trade secret violation could have occurred since no confidentiality agreement existed between it and Forest Laboratories (P) regarding information provided by Forest (P) to Pillsbury (D).

CONCISE RULE OF LAW: A confidentiality agreement is not necessary for a cause of action for violation of trade secrets to exist.

FACTS: Tidy House Corporation marketed on effervescent sweetener tablet. The tablet was manufactured and packaged by Forest Laboratories, Inc. (P). In 1964, Pillsbury (D), which had purchased Tidy House, discontinued its relationship with Forest (D) and engaged Formulations, Inc. (D) to manufacture and package the tablets. Forest (P) later sued Pillsbury (D), contending that its employees had divulged its packaging technique to the new contractor, which constituted improper use of trade secrets. It brought an action seeking injunctive relief and damages. Pillsbury (D) argued that no confidentiality agreement regarding the packaging technique existed, although it appeared that it had been implicitly understood that such information was to be kept confidential.

ISSUE: Is a confidentiality agreement necessary for a cause of action for violation of trade secrets to exist?

HOLDING AND DECISION: (Gordon, J.) No. A confidentiality agreement is not necessary for a cause of action for violation of trade secrets to exist. A cause of action for improper use of trade secrets exists when (1) information actually constitutes a trade secret, and (2) a confidential relationship existed with respect to the information. [The court first analyzed the information in question and concluded that some of it constituted trade secrets, and then turned to the issue of confidentiality.] For improper use of trade secrets to have occurred, the relationship under which the information was divulged must have been confidential. Contrary to Pillsbury's (D) assertions, no explicit confidentiality agreement is necessary for a violation to have occurred. As long as the circumstances under which the information was divulged show that the parties understood the information to be confidential, the necessary confidential relationship existed. Here, it appears that the parties did understand that the communications were to have been confidential, so a violation did occur. [The court went on to deny injunctive relief and award damages.]

EDITOR'S ANALYSIS: The court here largely based its decision on the Restatement of Torts §§ 757 and 758, which covered trade secrets. These sections were dropped in the 1979 second edition of the Restatement. The deletion was based on the belief that unfair competition was its own body of law that no longer belonged in torts. This deletion had no impact on the analysis of a trade secrets cause of action.

E.I. DUPONT deNEMOURS & CO. v. CHRISTOPHER

431 F.2d 1012 (5th Cir. 1970).

NATURE OF CASE: Appeal of denial of motion to dismiss action to enjoin use of trade secrets.

FACT SUMMARY: The Christophers (D) obtained trade secrets of E.I. DuPont (P) without engaging in fraudulent or illegal conduct.

CONCISE RULE OF LAW: One may be found to have improperly acquired another's trade secrets without having committed illegal or fraudulent conduct.

FACTS: E.I. DuPont deNemours & Co. (P) was in the process of constructing a fuel refinery when the Christophers (D) were found to have been taking aerial photographs of the facility while under construction. Contending that a trained observer could divine certain trade secrets from the photographs of the uncompleted facilities, DuPont (P) brought an action seeking to enjoin the distribution and use of the photographs. The Christophers (D) moved for dismissal under F.R.C.P. 12(b)(6), the federal equivalent of a general demurrer. This was denied, and the Christophers (D) instituted an interlocutory appeal.

ISSUE: May one be found to have improperly acquired another's trade secrets without having committed illegal or fraudulent conduct?

HOLDING AND DECISION: (Goldberg, J.) Yes. One may be found to have improperly acquired another's trade secrets without having committed illegal or fraudulent conduct. Most cases involving trade secrets do involve such conduct, examples being trespass or violation of a confidentiality agreement. However, it has never been the rule that acquisition of the secret must be through illegal or fraudulent conduct. All that is required is that the secret be discovered through improper means. In the context of discovering another's trade secrets, proper means consist of analysis of another's product and "backwards engineering" to determine how it was created. Industrial espionage is not such a proper means. Here, although the Christophers (D) did nothing illegal, they still used an information acquisition method that was improper. Thus, DuPont's (P) complaint did state facts sufficient to constitute a cause of action. Affirmed.

EDITOR'S ANALYSIS: The court spoke of "backwards engineering." This term refers to research which takes the final product and looks backward to try to ascertain the ingredients and techniques that produced it. In practice, the line between backward engineering and industrial espionage is not always clear.

NOTES:

WEXLER v. GREENBERG

Pa. Sup. Ct., 399 Pa. 569, 160 A.2d 430 (1960).

NATURE OF CASE: Appeal of injunction and award of damages for improper use of trade secrets.

FACT SUMMARY: Greenberg (D), former employee of Buckingham Wax Co. (P), used formulas he developed at Buckingham (P) in products manufactured by his new employer.

CONCISE RULE OF LAW: One does not improperly appropriate trade secrets from his employer if he developed the information in question.

FACTS: Greenberg (D) was a senior chemist for Buckingham Wax Co. (P), which manufactured household cleaning products. He later changed his employment to Brite Products Co. (D), which had heretofore only distributed such products, mostly those manufactured by Buckingham (P). After Greenberg (D) joined the company, it began manufacturing cleaning products. Some of these products utilized formulas developed by Greenberg (D) while at Buckingham (P) and incorporated by the latter in its products. Buckingham (P) brought an action for injunctive relief and damages, alleging misuse of trade secrets. The trial court issued an injunction and awarded damages, and an appeal was taken.

ISSUE: Does one improperly appropriate trade secrets from his employer if he developed the information in question?

HOLDING AND DECISION: (Cohen, J.) No. One does not improperly appropriate trade secrets from his employer if he developed the information in question. While the law recognizes the right of a businessman to be protected against the unfair usurpation of his trade secrets, it also recognizes the right of the individual to engage in the unhampered pursuit of the livelihood for which he is best suited. Traditionally, the law has tended to give greater weight to the latter interest, and the protection of trade secrets in the face of this interest will be narrow. In this context, it must be remembered that a trade secret action involves a breach of confidence. This occurs when the employer imparts some sort of information to the employee. Where, on the other hand, the employee developed the information, his later use thereof cannot be said to have violated a confidential relationship. Here, since the formulas at issue were developed by Greenberg (D), his later use of them did not constitute improper use of trade secrets. Reversed.

EDITOR'S ANALYSIS: It is not uncommon that an issue may develop as to who has a proprietary right in an employee's inventions and developments, and how far these rights go. As this case shows, the mere fact that the information was developed while the employee worked for the employer does not make the employer the sole owner thereof. For this reason, many such employers protect themselves with confidentiality agreements.

NOTES:

REED, ROBERTS ASSOCIATES, INC. v. STRAUMAN

N.Y. Ct. App., 40 N.Y.2d 303 (1976).

NOTES:

NATURE OF CASE: Appeal of injunction enforcing a covenant not to compete.

FACT SUMMARY: Reed, Roberts (P) sought to enforce a covenant not to compete executed by Strauman (D), despite the fact that Strauman's (D) services had not been extraordinary or unique.

CONCISE RULE OF LAW: An employee's covenant not to compete is not enforceable if the employee's services were not extraordinary or unique.

FACTS: Reed, Roberts Associates (P) was a firm engaged in providing advice to businesses in how to minimize worker's compensation costs. It hired Strauman (D) in 1962. Strauman (D) signed a covenant not to compete in the business in the New York City area for three years after ceasing employment with Reed, Roberts (P). In 1973, Strauman (D), now a vice president, left Reed, Roberts' (P) employ and formed his own company, engaged in the same business. Reed, Roberts (P) brought an action seeking to enforce the restrictive covenant. The trial court declined to enjoin Strauman (D) from engaging in business in competition with Reed, Roberts (P), but enjoined him from soliciting its clients. The appellate division affirmed, and both sides appealed.

ISSUE: Is an employee's covenant not to compete enforceable if the employee's services had not been extraordinary or unique?

HOLDING AND DECISION: (Wachtler, J.) No. An employee's covenant not to compete is not enforceable if the employee's services had not been extraordinary or unique. A covenant not to compete will only be enforced if it is reasonable. In the context of an employee, as opposed to a selling proprietor, courts carefully scrutinize the reasonableness of such contracts. Realizing that enforcing such a covenant interfere's with a person's ability to earn a living, the rule has been fashioned that only if the services of the employee were somehow unique or extraordinary will his former employer have such an interest in his subsequent employment that enforcing restrictions thereon could be called reasonable. Here, although Strauman (D) was corporate vice president, no evidence existed that his services were extraordinary or unique, and the trial court properly declined to enjoin him. [The court went on to hold that trade secret principles did not prohibit Strauman (D) from soliciting clients of Reed, Roberts (P), and reversed this aspect of the order.]

EDITOR'S ANALYSIS: Covenants not to compete are fairly common in the business world. Generally speaking, they fall into two categories. The first is when a proprietor sells a business. The second involves employment relationships. Neither case is particularly well-favored in the law, but the latter situation is the least favored of the two.

TABOR v. HOFFMAN

N.Y. Ct. App., 118 N.Y. 30, 23 N.E. 12 (2d Div. 1889).

NATURE OF CASE: Appeal of injunction against product manufacture.

FACT SUMMARY: Hoffman (D) began manufacturing pumps based on unpublished specifications belonging to Tabor (P).

CONCISE RULE OF LAW: Product specifications improperly obtained may not be incorporated into a product, even if the specifications have already been incorporated into a product on the market.

FACTS: Tabor (P) manufactured a commercially successful pump. He had never patented it, and the specifications he kept secret. At one point Tabor (P) took certain component patterns into one Walz for repair. Walz surreptitiously copied the patterns and sold them to Hoffman (D), who began manufacturing pumps based on the specification. Tabor (P) obtained an order enjoining Hoffman (D) from such manufacture and Hoffman (D) appealed.

ISSUE: May product specifications improperly obtained be incorporated into a product if the specifications have already been incorporated into a product already on the market?

HOLDING AND DECISION: (Vann, J.) No. Product specifications improperly obtained may not be incorporated into a product, even if the specifications have already been incorporated into a product already on the market. Information regarding a nonpatented product is the property of the party generating that information until such time as he chooses to publish it. While the manufacture and marketing of a product incorporating that information to some extent makes the information less secret, the sale of such an article is not the publication of the formula or device used in its manufacture. Here, had Hoffman (D) managed to figure out the pump's design by examining the pump, he would have acted properly. However, to design a pump based on pirated designs constituted improper use of trade secrets. Affirmed.

DISSENT: (Follett, C.J.) The invention was not the patterns, but the pump itself. By marketing the pump, Tabor (P) had lost the exclusive right to use the information which went into the making of the pump.

EDITOR'S ANALYSIS: Whether to patent or not to patent is a question that any inventor of a new product must make. The upside of a patent is that it will give the holder thereof a monopoly for a period of time. However, the downside is that the patent is public information. Here, the pump had originally been patented. The patent had expired, and Tabor (P) made certain improvements which he had elected not to patent.

NOTES:

KEWANEE OIL CO. v. BICON CORP.

416 U.S. 470 (1974).

NATURE OF CASE: Review of order dissolving injunction against disclosure of trade secrets.

FACT SUMMARY: Bicon Corp. (D) contended that federal patent law preempted Ohio trade secret law.

CONCISE RULE OF LAW: Federal law does not preempt state trade secret law.

FACTS: Certain employees of Kewanee Oil Co. (P), who had signed confidentiality agreements while employed at Kewanee (P), began working for Bicon Corp (D). Bicon (D) soon thereafter began manufacturing a certain kind of synthetic crystal used in radiation detection. Kewanee (P), which considered its unpatented process in making these crystals to be a trade secret, brought an injunction seeking to enjoin Bicon (D) from using information learned from its ex-employees to make the crystals. A district court issued such an injunction. The Sixth Circuit reversed, holding that federal patent law preempted Ohio trade secret law. The Supreme Court granted review.

ISSUE: Does federal patent law preempt state trade secret law?

HOLDING AND DECISION: (Burger, C.J.) No. Federal patent law does not preempt state trade secret law. It is well established that states are free to regulate the area of intellectual property, provided that such regulations do not conflict with applicable federal law. In the area of federal patent law and its state law equivalent, trade secret protection, Congress has not explicitly mandated preemption. Therefore, preemption will be found only if state trade secret law interferes with the policies underlying patent law. The purpose of patent law is to promote invention, as is the purpose of trade secret law. Since their goals do not conflict, the question becomes whether the two laws conflict in operation. As an initial matter, trade secret law is broader than patent law; many things which may be trade secrets are not patentable. Clearly there is no conflict in this context, as trade secret law takes nothing from patent law. In cases where a certain trade secret is also patentable, the potential for conflict is greater. Nonetheless, this Court believes the conflict to be minimal. Granted, patent law mandates disclosure of the patent process, while trade secrets involve nondisclosure. Nonetheless, the advantages of a patent on a product or process are so great that, as a matter of practicality, one possessing a patentable product or process will almost always opt for the patent. The only likely result of declaring trade secret law preempted would be to encourage frivolous patent applications and to promote extensive intracompany secrecy, neither of which is socially desirable. For these reasons, patent law does not preempt state trade secret law. Reversed.

CONCURRENCE: (Marshall, J.) While the Court is incorrect in assuming that inventors will almost always opt for a patent over trade secret protection, nothing indicates that Congress intended to coerce inventors to go the route of patents rather than trade secrets.

DISSENT: (Douglas, J.) Congress in the patent laws has declared that every article not covered by a valid patent is within the public domain. State trade secret law undercuts this intent.

EDITOR'S ANALYSIS: A patent application requires disclosure of the essential features of a product. If a product is patented, this information becomes public. While an inventor can be somewhat selective about the information provided to the patent office, sufficient information must be provided to make the product "work." For this reason, a patent almost always makes the keeping of a trade secret impossible.

NOTES:

CARSON v. HERE'S JOHNNY PORTABLE TOILETS, INC.

698 F.2d 831, 218 U.S.P.Q. 1 (6th Cir. 1983).

NATURE OF CASE: Appeal of dismissal of action to enjoin trade name use.

FACT SUMMARY: Carson (P), a well-known television personality, objected to the use of a term identified with him, even though neither his name nor image was used.

CONCISE RULE OF LAW: A celebrity may enjoin the use of a phrase associated with him, even if neither his name nor likeness is used.

FACTS: Johnny Carson (P) was the host of the "Tonight" show on television since 1962 (and until 1992). Over the years, the phrase by which he was introduced, "Here's Johnny," had become associated with him. In 1976, Here's Johnny Portable Toilets, Inc. (D), which operated a portable toilet business, began operating under the name "Here's Johnny." Carson (P) brought an action to enjoin use of the phrase as a trade name, alleging unfair competition and violation of the right of privacy. The district court dismissed all causes of action, and Carson appealed.

ISSUE: May a celebrity enjoin the use of a phrase associated with him, even if neither his name nor likeness is used?

HOLDING AND DECISION: (Brown, J.) Yes. A celebrity may enjoin the use of a phrase associated with him, even if neither his name nor likeness is used. The law recognizes a right to privacy, of which one component is what has been characterized as a right to publicity. Essentially, this doctrine holds that a celebrity's "celebrity" is a property right, and no one may exploit that right for his own gain. Although cases involving this right generally involve names or images, no reason exists for not extending it to any other form of identification. If a certain phrase has come to be associated with a celebrity, he has a property interest in that phrase. Here, it is undisputed that the phrase "Here's Johnny" is firmly imbedded in the public mind as synonymous with Carson (P), so his right to use the phrase may not be appropriated.

DISSENT: (Kennedy, J.) The right of publicity may only go so far as his name, likeness, or an actual performance. To extend it to phrases would allow a person to use a common expression to the point he becomes associated with it, and then remove it from the public domain. This is an unacceptable result. Beyond questions of fairness it conflicts with the federal policy against monopolies and favoring free expression.

EDITOR'S ANALYSIS: The right of publicity is relatively new, being developed more recently than other areas of intellectual property law. It was first described in detail by Prosser in 1960. Today, about half the jurisdictions recognize the right. In California, the center of the entertainment industry, the right is recognized by statute.

NOTES:

ZACCHINI v. SCRIPPS-HOWARD BROADCASTING CO.

433 U.S. 562, 205 U.S.P.Q. 741 (1977).

NATURE OF CASE: Appeal from denial of damages for infringement of "right of publicity."

FACT SUMMARY: Scripps-Howard's (D) newscast of Zacchini's (P) performance as a "human cannonball" was found to be constitutionally privileged by the Ohio Supreme Court, in spite of the fact that the court recognized the telecast to be an unauthorized invasion of Zacchini's (P) right of publicity.

CONCISE RULE OF LAW: The First and Fourteenth Amendments do not immunize the media from liability when they broadcast a performer's entire act without his consent.

FACTS: Zacchini (P), an entertainer, performs a 15-second "human cannonball" act in which he is shot from a cannon into a net 200 feet away. While performing at a county fair in Ohio, a freelance reporter for Scripps-Howard (D) videotaped the entire act without Zacchini's (P) consent. The film clip was shown on an 11 o'clock news program that night, together with favorable commentary. Zacchini (P) brought an action for damages, alleging that Scripps-Howard's (D) conduct was an unlawful appropriation of his professional property. The trial court granted Scripps-Howard's (D) motion for summary judgment but the court of appeals reversed, agreeing that the First Amendment did not privilege the press to show the entire performance without compensating Zacchini (P) for his financial injury. On appeal to the Ohio Supreme Court, Zacchini's (P) right of publicity was acknowledged but judgment was granted for Scripps--Howard (D) on the basis that the news broadcast was protected by the First Amendment. Certiorari was granted by the U.S. Supreme Court.

ISSUE: Do the First and Fourteenth Amendments immunize the media from liability for infringement of a performer's state-law "right of publicity"?

HOLDING AND DECISION: (White, J.) No. "Wherever the line in particular situations is to be drawn between media reports that are protected and those that are not, the First and Fourteenth Amendments do not immunize the media when they broadcast a performer's entire act without his consent." To broadcast a film of such an act poses a substantial threat to the economic value of that performance. Here, the economic value of Zacchini's (P) act lay in his right of exclusive control over the publicity given his performance. Although Scripps-Howard (D) knew that Zacchini (P) objected to having his act televised, they nevertheless displayed the entire film. It is only logical that people would thereafter be less willing to pay to see the act at the fair. In this case, Ohio has recognized the appropriation of the very activity by which Zacchini (P) acquired his reputation in the first place. Although it is true that entertainment itself can be important news and that entertainment, as well as news, enjoys First Amendment protection, Zacchini (P) does not seek to enjoin the broadcast of his performance. He simply wants to be paid for it. The Constitution does not prevent Ohio from requiring Scripps-Howard (D) to compensate Zacchini (P) for broadcasting his act on television, just as it would not privilege Scripps-Howard (D) to film and broadcast a copyrighted dramatic work without liability to the copyright owner. Reversed.

DISSENT: (Powell, J.) For a routine portion of a regular news program, it should be held that the First Amendment protects the station from a "right of publicity" or "appropriation" suit, absent a strong showing by the plaintiff that the news broadcast was a subterfuge or cover for private or commercial exploitation.

DISSENT: (Stevens, J.) The basis of the state court's holding is sufficiently doubtful as to whether it rests entirely on federal constitutional grounds to warrant being remanded for clarification before the federal constitutional issue is decided.

EDITOR'S ANALYSIS: The standard articulated by the majority, i.e., broadcasting an entire performance, is workable in its basic form, in that the court must merely determine whether the broadcast was or was not of the performer's entire act. Even so, this standard is open to abuse by broadcasters who simply cut a few seconds off an act when it is televised. The essence of the act may be shown but if it is not the entire act, the broadcaster is protected from liability by the First Amendment. If the intent of the court is to protect a performer's "economic value" in his performance, a more definitive standard should be applied. The "entire act" standard was sufficient here but its application in future cases may serve to protect broadcasters even though the economic consequences to the performer may be the same a those suffered by Zacchini (P).

NOTES:

BLUE BELL, INC. v. FARAH MFG. CO.

508 F.2d 1260, 185 U.S.P.Q. 1 (5th Cir. 1975).

NATURE OF CASE: Appeal of order enjoining use of trademark.

NOTES:

FACT SUMMARY: Farah Mfg. Co. (D) sought to use an internal shipment of clothing bearing a trademark as a basis for a claimed first use of the mark.

CONCISE RULE OF LAW: An internal shipment of a product bearing a trademark may not form the basis of a first use of the mark.

FACTS: In 1973 Blue Bell, Inc. (P) and Farah Mfg. Co. (D) brought out a line of clothing under the name "Time Out." On July 3 of that year, Farah (D) shipped one pair of Time Out pants to each of its sales managers. On July 5, Blue Bell (P) shipped several hundred pairs in an intracompany transaction. Farah (D) started selling to the public in September, and Blue Bell (P) began doing so in October. Blue Bell (P) brought a suit seeking to enjoin Farah (D) from using the label. Farah (D) counterclaimed for similar relief. A district court entered judgment for Farah (D), and Blue Bell (P) appealed, contending that Farah's (D) July 3 shipment to have been too small to be considered.

ISSUE: May an internal shipment of a product bearing a trademark form the basis of a first use of the mark?

HOLDING AND DECISION: (Gewin, J.) No. An internal shipment of a product bearing a trademark may not form the basis of a first use of the mark. The primary, perhaps singular purpose of a trademark is to provide a means for the consumer to separate or distinguish one manufacturer's goods from those of another. Personnel within a company can identify an item by its style number or other unique code. Trademarks are, therefore, relevant only in the context of the public's involvement with a product. Intracompany shipments of any size are not to be considered in determining when a trademark was first used. Here, not only was Farah's (D) July 3 shipment intracompany, but so was Blue Bell's (P) larger shipment. For these reasons, neither may be used as a basis for determining first use. Therefore, since Farah (D) first commenced sales to the general public, its use of the mark had priority. Affirmed.

EDITOR'S ANALYSIS: Trademark law has both federal and state components. Federal trademark registration is afforded under the Lanham Act, codified at 15 U.S.C. § 1125. In this case, neither party had applied for federal registration, so state law applied. In this case, federal and state law regarding priority did not substantially differ.

MANHATTAN INDUSTRIES INC. v. SWEATER BEE BY BANFF
627 F.2d 628, 207 U.S.P.Q. 89 (2nd Cir. 1980).

NATURE OF CASE: Appeal of order enjoining use of trademark.

NOTES:

FACT SUMMARY: Sweater Bee (D) was beaten by a short margin of time by Manhattan Industries (P) in a race to adopt an abandoned trademark.

CONCISE RULE OF LAW: One slightly losing a race to adopt an abandoned trademark does not necessarily lose the right to use the mark.

FACTS: General Mills, Inc. had recently abandoned a clothing trademark called "Kimberly." Notice of such abandonment was published May 7, 1979. On May 9, Manhattan Industries, Inc.'s (P) predecessor began shipping merchandise bearing the label "Kimberly." Sweater Bee by Banff, Inc. (D) began shipping clothing with the same name May 10. Manhattan (P) brought an action seeking to enjoin Sweater Bee (D) from further manufacture and for damages. Sweater Bee (D) counterclaimed for the same relief. The trial court granted an injunction in favor of Manhattan (P) on the basis of its priority, and Sweater Bee (D) appealed.

ISSUE: Does one slightly losing a race to adopt an abandoned trademark necessarily lose the right to use the mark?

HOLDING AND DECISION: (Lumbard, J.) No. One slightly losing a race to adopt an abandoned trademark does not necessarily lose the right to use the mark. The concept of priority in the law of trademarks is applied not in its calendar sense but on the basis of the equities involved. Where no bad faith is shown, it would be inequitable to penalize a party who has invested time and money in a mark because of a difference of a few days in the marketing of the marked product. Here, the behavior of both parties appears to have been in good faith, and to allow Manhattan (P) to exclude Sweater Bee's (D) use of a nonoriginal trademark would not be equitable. Rather, an order should be fashioned mandating that both parties contrive to use the mark, but in manners sufficiently distinct that consumer confusion is not likely. Reversed.

EDITOR'S ANALYSIS: Abandonment of a mark can occur in two basic manners. The first, employed by General Mills here, is explicit abandonment. It can also be abandoned by nonuse. Section 4 of the Lanham Act, codified at 15 U.S.C. § 1127, creates a reputable presumption of abandonment if a mark is not used for two years.

DELAWARE & HUDSON CANAL CO. v. CLARK

80 U.S. 311 (1871).

NATURE OF CASE: Review of order dismissing trademark infringement action.

FACT SUMMARY: Delaware & Hudson Canal Co. (P) sought to appropriate by trademark the geographical area from which its product, coal, was furnished.

CONCISE RULE OF LAW: A party may not appropriate through a trademark the description of the geographical source of his product.

FACTS: Delaware & Hudson Canal Co. (P) produced coal from the Luckawanna Valley, which it called "Luckawanna Coal." Clark (D) subsequently began extracting coal from the same area, which it also called Luckawanna Coal. Delaware & Hudson (P) brought an action to enjoin the use of the name. The court of appeals dismissed the complaint, and Delaware & Hudson (P) appealed.

ISSUE: May a party appropriate through a trademark the description of the geographical source of his product?

HOLDING AND DECISION: (Strong, J.) No. A party may not appropriate through a trademark the description of the geographical source of his product. The basic wrong that trademark law seeks to avoid is one party selling his product as that of another, which is to say, as something that it is not. A name which is descriptive of the generic type of product involved does not pass off the product as something it is not, even if another product incorporates the name. This is equally true of geographical names. Here, Clark's (D) "Luckawanna Coal" was no less Luckawanna coal than Delaware & Hudson's (P) "Luckawanna Coal," and therefore no trademark violation occurred. Affirmed.

EDITOR'S ANALYSIS: One of the basic requirements of trademark law is distinctiveness. In order to be eligible to be a trademark, both the product and the trademark must be distinctive in some manner. If a mark did not identify a singly source of a product, the purpose of enforcing trademark law would not exist. Further, to allow the trademarking of generic names would encourage monopolization, in contravention to stated policy.

NOTES:

KING-SEELEY THERMOS CO. v. ALADDIN INDUSTRIES, INC.
321 F.2d 577, 138 U.S.P.Q. 349 (2d Cir. 1963).

NATURE OF CASE: Appeal of injunction setting trademark rights.

FACT SUMMARY: A district court found the word "Thermos" to have acquired a generic meaning and therefore not to be an enforceable trademark.

CONCISE RULE OF LAW: A trademark that acquires a generic meaning is no longer enforceable.

FACTS: In 1907 King-Seeley Thermos Co. (P) began marketing a vacuum-insulated liquid container under the name "Thermos." In the early 1960s Aladdin Industries (D) began marketing a container with the name "Thermos" in it. King-Seeley (P) brought an action seeking to enjoin use of the name. The district court, finding that most of the public had come to associate the word "thermos" as a generic description of vacuum liquid containers, declined to enjoin its use. The court's order merely mandated that Aladdin (D) not try to pass off its thermos as the original Thermos. King-Seeley (P) appealed.

ISSUE: Is a trademark that acquires a generic meaning enforceable?

HOLDING AND DECISION: (Moore, J.) No. A trademark that acquires a generic meaning is no longer enforceable. With respect to trademarks, the ultimate question is what the public understands when a word is used. If the public understands that word to mean a particular brand of a product, that word is a valid trademark. If the public, on the other hand, believes the word to describe the type of product it represents, then the name is generic and a trademark may not be enforced. That is true no matter what steps a manufacturer may have taken to avoid this result. Once a trademark is appropriated by the public, it is no longer a trademark. Here, the district court found the word "Thermos" to have acquired a generic meaning, and this is supported by the record. Affirmed.

EDITOR'S ANALYSIS: The rule stated above presents an innovative party with the danger of becoming a victim of its own success. If a party manages to get the public to identify a product with its own brand, the brand name may lose its distinctiveness. History abounds with brand names that eventually became generic. Examples include "aspirin" and "cellophane."

NOTES:

IN RE N.A.D., INC.

754 F.2d 996, 224 U.S.P.Q. 969 (Fed. Cir. 1985).

NATURE OF CASE: Appeal of Patent and Trademark Office refusal to register a trademark.

FACT SUMMARY: A product for which N.A.D., Inc. sought a trademark was a very different product from another product having a similar, registered name.

CONCISE RULE OF LAW: A name similar to a trademarked name may be registered if the products are dissimilar.

FACTS: N.A.D., Inc. produced a large machine for use by anesthesiologists during surgery. It sought to register as a trademark the product name "Narkomed." The Patent and Trademark Office refused to register the name. A medical consultation service was already registered as Narco Medical Services, and a manufacturer of medical equipment, including an anesthesia machine, was called Narco. The Narco anesthesia machine was very different from N.A.D.'s. Nonetheless, the Patent Office refused to register the name, due to the similarities with the already-registered products and services. The Board of Patent Appeals affirmed, and N.A.D. appealed.

ISSUE: May a name similar to a trademarked name be registered if the products are dissimilar?

HOLDING AND DECISION: (Rich, J.) Yes. A name similar to a trademarked name may be registered if the products are dissimilar. A trademark application should be denied if it is likely that confusion between the products is likely to occur. While similarity of names is a factor, it is not determinative. If the products are sufficiently dissimilar that confusion is not likely to result, registration is appropriate. The sophistication of the ultimate user is important in this regard; the more sophisticated the user, the less dissimilar the products must be to be distinct. Here, the names involved, Narkomed and Narco, both involved an anesthesia device. At first glance, these seem unacceptably similar. However, the machines involved are very different in design. Further, the ultimate users of such machines are doctors, a sophisticated buying public. For these reasons, a danger of confusion sufficient to justify refusing registration. Reversed.

EDITOR'S ANALYSIS: In this instance, the prior parties had in fact given N.A.D. permission to use the name "Narkomed." Despite this, the Patent Office still refused to register the name. While agreement by parties involved may be evidence of no danger of confusion, the Patent Office is not bound by the parties' agreement. If it disagrees, it may still disallow registration.

NOTES:

IN RE SUN OIL CO.

U.S.C.C.P.A., 426 F.2d 401, 165 U.S.P.Q. 718 (1970).

NATURE OF CASE: Appeal of denial of trademark registration.

FACT SUMMARY: Sun Oil sought to register as a trademark "Custom Blended" for a brand of gasoline, which the Patent Office declined on the basis that it was merely a descriptive term.

CONCISE RULE OF LAW: A name that is a mere description cannot be registered as a trademark.

FACTS: Sun Oil Co. offered a type of gasoline that was blended, at the request of the purchaser, from several grades of gasoline. Sun Oil sought to register "Custom Blended" as a trademark. The Patent Office refused registration, holding the name to be merely descriptive of the product. Sun Oil appealed.

ISSUE: Can a name that is a mere description be registered as a trademark?

HOLDING AND DECISION: (Almund, J.) No. A name that is a mere description cannot be registered as a trademark; 15 U.S.C. § 1052(f) requires that for a name to be given a trademark registration it must be distinctive of the applicant's goods and no one else's. This is sometimes termed as having a "secondary meaning." A name that merely describes a product cannot fit this definition, as it can also be used to describe a similar product not put out by the applicant. Here, the Patent Office found the term "Custom Blended" to be merely descriptive of its nature. This conclusion seems completely correct, and for that reason registration was properly denied. Affirmed.

CONCURRENCE: (Rich, J.) The name for which registration was requested was so highly descriptive of the product that it is incapable of acquiring a secondary meaning.

DISSENT: (Fisher, J.) Evidence exists that Sun Oil has heavily promoted "Custom Blended" gasoline over 12 years, and the public has come to associate the term with Sun Oil. This being so, the product has come to have a secondary meaning and therefore can be registered.

EDITOR'S ANALYSIS: "Secondary meaning" is an exception to the general rule that a description cannot be registered. It is possible that a description will become so closely linked with a product or a manufacturer that the name comes to mean that product or manufacturer. When this occurs, the name has acquired a secondary meaning and may be registered.

NOTES:

IN RE LOEW'S THEATRES, INC.

769 F.2d 764, 226 U.S.P.Q. 865 (Fed. Cir. 1985).

NATURE OF CASE: Appeal of denial of trademark registration.

FACT SUMMARY: A tobacco product called "Durango" was denied registration on the basis of the that the name would lead to the incorrect belief by the public that the product came Durango, Mexico.

CONCISE RULE OF LAW: Registration will be denied if a product's name will give a false impression as to its place of origin.

FACTS: Loew's Theatres, Inc. submitted an application for registration of the name "Durango" for a line of chewing tobacco. The Patent Office, finding that Durango, Mexico, produced tobacco (including chewing tobacco) and that the tobacco for the product in question did not come from the region, denied the application. The Trademarks Trial and Appeal Board affirmed, and Loew's appealed.

ISSUE: Will registration be denied if a product's name will give a false impression as to its place of origin?

HOLDING AND DECISION: (Nies, J.) Yes. Registration will be denied if a product's name will give a false impression as to its place of origin. Under § 2(e)(2) of the Lanham Act, when a product name is primarily of a misdescriptive geographical character, registration will be disallowed. While parties are free to use geographical names for their products, they cannot do so in such a manner as to give a false impression as to the origin of the product. A name which does this will not be registered. Here, the Patent Office found that Durango, Mexico, is a sizable area that is known to a large number of Americans, and it also produces tobacco. From this it concluded that use of the name "Durango" would mislead the public into believing that the tobacco came from Durango, Mexico, which it did not. The factual findings were not clearly erroneous, and the legal conclusions reached by the Patent Office therefrom were correct. Affirmed.

EDITOR'S ANALYSIS: A place need not be particularly well-known as the origin of a product for § 2(e)(2) to apply. The issue is whether a name will falsely suggest a place of origin. The notoriety of a location for producing a type of product will be a factor in this analysis, but only that. Here, for instance, Durango, Mexico, was not especially well known for its tobacco.

NOTES:

IN RE CARSON

Trademark Trial and App. Bd., 197 U.S.P.Q. 554 (1977).

NATURE OF CASE: Appeal of denial of trademark application.

FACT SUMMARY: Entertainer Johnny Carson sought to register his name as a trademark.

CONCISE RULE OF LAW: An individual's name may be registered as a trademark.

FACTS: John W. Carson, a prominent television entertainer, was generally known as Johnny Carson. He would use the name "Johnny" in connection with all concerts, appearances, and other publicity. He applied for registration of "Johnny Carson" as a trademark. The Patent and Trademark Office rejected his application on the basis that the name served as personal identification only, and Carson appealed.

ISSUE: May an individual's name be registered as a trademark?

HOLDING AND DECISION: (Rice, M.) Yes. An individual's name may be registered as a trademark. A name, whether it be that of an individual company, or anything else, may not be registered as a trademark if its only purpose is identification. However, a name which not only identifies a person but also identifies goods or services may be trademarked, whether the name is of a company or of a natural person. Here, Carson has used the name "Johnny Carson" in conjunction with advertisements for concerts and appearances. This being so, the name has been used to identify not only Carson himself but his services as well. For this reason, the name "Johnny Carson" may be trademarked. Reversed.

EDITOR'S ANALYSIS: The Board came to the opposite conclusion in In re Lee Trevino Enterprises, 182 U.S.P.Q. 253 (1974). There, professional golfer Lee Trevino was denied a registration for his name. In that case, however, no evidence of association with a service or product was produced. Trademark application cases tend to be very fact-specific, and the precedential value of any such case must be analyzed with this in mind.

NOTES:

EX PARTE HANDMACHER-VOGEL, INC.

Comm. of Patents, 98 U.S.P.Q. 413 (1953).

NATURE OF CASE: Appeal of denial of service mark registration application.

NOTES:

FACT SUMMARY: Handmacher-Vogel, Inc. sought to register as a service mark the name "Weathervane," a name which was connected to a line of products it produced.

CONCISE RULE OF LAW: That a mark is also connected with a product will not prevent the mark from being registerable as a service mark.

FACTS: Handmacher-Vogel, Inc. manufactured and distributed a line of clothing under the label "Weathervane." At one point it began sponsoring a tournament for professional women golfers, in which the name "Weathervane" was featured prominently in advertisements. Stores carrying Weathervane clothing were encouraged to exploit the promotional opportunities afforded by the tournament. Handmacher-Vogel sought to register the word "Weathervane" as a service mark. The trademark examiner denied the application on the basis that the name related to goods, not a service. Handmacher-Vogel appealed.

ISSUE: Will a mark's connection with a product prevent the mark from being registerable as a service mark?

HOLDING AND DECISION: (Leeds, Asst. Comm.) No. That a mark is also connected with a product will not prevent the mark from being registerable as a service mark. A mark used by a person in connection with services which arise incidentally to the sale of goods may not be registered as a service mark. However, a producer of goods which offers a bona fide service is not precluded from registering the name given to the service as a service mark, even if the name is the same as that given to the goods. Here, the name "Weathervane" was given to a golf tournament, which was thoroughly promoted. The tournament was an activity quite separate from selling clothing, although there was an obvious marketing connection. Because the tournament was a service activity quite apart from selling clothing, "Weathervane" was registerable as a service mark. Reversed.

EDITOR'S ANALYSIS: In this instance, "Weathervane" was already a registered trademark in connection with the clothing. It appears that the trademark examiner had been under the belief that a mark could not be registered as both a trade and service mark. This conclusion was incorrect, as the reversal indicates.

IN RE FLORIDA CITRUS COMM'N

Trademark Trial and App. Bd., 160 U.S.P.Q. 495 (1968).

NATURE OF CASE: Appeal of denial of application for certification mark registration.

FACT SUMMARY: The Florida Citrus Commission, which held a certain trademark, attempted to register the same mark as a certification mark.

CONCISE RULE OF LAW: The holder of a trade or service mark may not register the same mark as a certification mark.

FACTS: The Florida Citrus Commission was a Florida corporation comprising an arm of the Florida government. Its purpose was to regulate, tax, control, and promote Florida citrus products. Pursuant to its promotional objectives, the commission created a distinctive mark bearing the words "The real thing o.j. from Florida." The mark was trademarked. Pursuant to its regulatory objectives, the commission, wishing to make the mark its stamp of approval, applied to register the mark as a certification mark. The application was rejected, and the commission appealed.

ISSUE: May the holder of a trade or service mark register the same mark as a certification mark?

HOLDING AND DECISION: (Lefkowitz, M.) No. The holder of a trade or service mark may not register the same mark as a certification mark. Section 14(e)(2) of the Lanham Act provides that a certification mark shall be cancelled as soon as a party holding that mark becomes involved in the process of actually marketing the type of goods covered by the certification mark. The purpose of this is to prevent a party from being in the position of certifying its own goods or services. Congress perceived that such practices could lead to monopolistic or other anticompetitive results and was to be discouraged. Since certification marks cannot continue when the holder thereof begins marketing a related product, it follows that one already engaged in marketing such a product cannot obtain a certification mark. One having a trademark covering a certain product is presumed to be engaged in the marketing of such a product. Here, the commission already had a trademark covering the goods to be certified and was without doubt engaged in the marketing of such products. The certification mark application was therefore properly rejected. Affirmed.

DISSENT: (Leach, M.) The statute at issue and legislative history are not at all clear on the point the majority decides.

EDITOR'S ANALYSIS: Certification marks are an unusual breed in trademark law. As the instant case shows, the mark cannot be used by one promoting the product involved. Rather, the mark is meant to imply an unbiased approval of a product or service. Examples include the seals of Good Housekeeping Magazine and Underwriters Laboratory.

NOTES:

IN RE OWENS-CORNING FIBERGLAS CORP.

774 F.2d 1116, 227 U.S.P.Q. 417 (Fed. Cir. 1985).

NATURE OF CASE: Appeal of denial of trademark application.

FACT SUMMARY: Owens-Corning Fiberglas Corp. sought to register as a trademark the color pink in connection with its fiberglass insulation product.

CONCISE RULE OF LAW: A color may be registered as a trademark.

FACTS: Owens-Corning Fiberglas Corp. had been marketing a pink fiberglass insulation product since 1956. For years prior to 1980 it had advertised the product, always noting its pink color in the advertisements. In 1980, it applied to register as a trademark the color pink in connection with insulation. The Patent and Trademark Office denied the application, and the Trademark Trial and Appeals Board affirmed. Owens-Corning appealed.

ISSUE: May a color be registered as a trademark?

HOLDING AND DECISION: (Newman, J.) Yes. A color may be registered as a trademark. The preamble to § 2 of the Lanham Act states that no trademark shall be refused registration on account of its nature, unless one or more specific exceptions to registrability exist. Here, the record makes it amply clear that Owens-Corning has expended considerable effort and money to promote its product, and that the color pink has figured prominently in its advertising. It appears that the public has come to associate pink insulation with Owens-Corning. For these reasons, the color pink was properly registerable as a trademark. Reversed.

DISSENT: (Bissell, J.) It has long been the rule that color is not registerable as a trademark. The Lanham Act does not by its terms change this rule, as numerous decisions based thereon demonstrate.

EDITOR'S ANALYSIS: The common law rule was that color was not capable of appropriation as a trademark. This rule was enunciated by the Supreme Court at least as early as 1906, in A. Leschen & Sons Rope Co. v. Broderick, 201 U.S. 166 (1906). The main fear was that allowing such could lead to monopolization. The Lanham Act was passed in 1946, and since that time courts have reached different results as to whether the Act abrogated the common law rule.

NOTES:

DAWN DONUT CO. v. HART'S FOOD STORES, INC.

267 F.2d 358, 121 U.S.P.Q. 430 (2d Cir. 1959).

NATURE OF CASE: Appeal of denial of injunction prohibiting product name use.

FACT SUMMARY: Dawn Donut Co. (P), which distributed doughnut mix under the name "Dawn" in an area of New York separate from Hart Food's (D) use of the name, sought to enjoin such use.

CONCISE RULE OF LAW: The holder of a registered trademark may not enjoin another's use thereof in a different market.

FACTS: Dawn Donut Co. (P) sold doughnut mix at the wholesale level in several states, including parts of New York. The buyers of the mixes were allowed to call themselves Dawn Donut Shops. Dawn (P) registered the name "Dawn" in connection with doughnuts. Subsequent to this, Hart's Food Stores, Inc. (D) began selling "Dawn Donuts" in six New York counties adjacent to Rochester. Dawn Donut Co. (P) did not distribute mix in this area. Dawn (P) brought an action seeking to enjoin Hart's (D) use of the name. The district court dismissed the action, and Dawn (P) appealed.

ISSUE: May the holder of a registered trademark enjoin another's use thereof in a different market?

HOLDING AND DECISION: (Lombard, J.) No. The holder of a registered trademark may not enjoin another's use thereof in a different market. The Lanham Act, 15 U.S.C. § 1114, sets out the standard for awarding a registrant relief against the unauthorized use of his mark by another. It provides that the registrant may enjoin only that concurrent use which creates a likelihood of confusion in the perception of the public as to the origin of the products in connection with the use of the products. Where the product markets overlap, the junior user's use of the mark may not be enjoined. Here, the district court found that the two markets involved did not overlap, and this finding was not clearly erroneous. The court was therefore correct in holding that an injunction should not issue. The action was properly dismissed, although if Dawn (P) ever expands into the area serviced by Hart (D), it may then seek the injunction denied here. Affirmed.

EDITOR'S ANALYSIS: At one time, Dawn (P) did operate in the area serviced by Hart (D), but had ceased doing so before Hart (D) commenced its operations. This, however, did not constitute abandonment. Under 15 U.S.C. § 1127, only abandonment at the retail level entirely can constitute abandonment. This left Dawn (P) free to reenter the area occupied by Hart (D).

NOTES:

SCARVES BY VERA, INC. v. TODO IMPORTS, LTD.

544 F.2d 1167, 192 U.S.P.Q. 289 (2d Cir. 1976).

NATURE OF CASE: Appeal of dismissal of action for equitable relief and damages for trademark infringement.

FACT SUMMARY: Scarves By Vera, Inc. (P), which had a trademark on its "Vera" line of clothing, sought to enjoin Todo Imports' (D) use of the designation on cosmetics and toiletries.

CONCISE RULE OF LAW: One who has a trademark on apparel may enjoin the mark's use on cosmetics and toiletries.

FACTS: In 1946, the predecessor of Scarves by Vera, Inc. (P) began marketing medium-to-high fashion women's apparel under the name "Vera," which was subsequently trademarked. These items were marketed for the most part in upscale retailers such as Bloomingdale's. By the 1970s Vera (P) products included not only women's apparel, but apartment accessories and linens as well. These were advertised in numerous periodicals and newspapers. In 1970, Todo Imports, Ltd. (D) began distributing a line of cosmetics and toiletries manufactured by Vera, S.A. of Spain. These products which also featured the name of their packaging were sold in many of the same retailers that featured Scarves by Vera's (P) products. Scarves by Vera, Inc. (P) brought an action seeking to enjoin Todo (D) from distributing products containing the name "Vera." The district court dismissed, and Scarves by Vera (P) appealed.

ISSUE: May one having a trademark on apparel enjoin the mark's use on cosmetics and toiletries?

HOLDING AND DECISION: (Lumbard, J.) Yes. One having a trademark on apparel may enjoin the mark's use on cosmetics and toiletries. Three identifiable trademark interests relate to such a situation. First, the senior user's interest in being able to enter a related field at some future time; second, his interest in protecting the mark's reputation from possible tarnishing by inferior merchandise; and third, the public's interest in avoiding product confusion. It is well established that a trademark covers not only competing goods, but related goods. It is well known that apparel makers can and have put out cosmetic lines under the same name. Cosmetics are, therefore, related to apparel. Scarves by Vera's (P) interest in possibly entering this field is infringed by the "Vera" products distributed by Todo (D). Further, as Todo's "Vera" products are sold by many of the same retailers as are Scarves by Vera's (P), the public's interest in avoiding confusion is impacted. Consequently, absent any clear equities favoring the junior marketer, Todo (D) in this instance, an injunction should issue in the circumstances presented here. Reversed.

EDITOR'S ANALYSIS: This case shows the potential withering away of the concept of abandonment. Traditionally, long nonuse would constitute abandonment of a trademark. Here, however, the mark had never been used by Scarves by Vera (P) with respect to cosmetics, yet the mark was upheld. This would seem somewhat at odds with the concept of abandonment.

NOTES:

MALTINA CORP. v. CAWY BOTTLING CO.
613 F.2d 582, 205 U.S.P.Q. 489 (5th Cir. 1980).

NATURE OF CASE: Appeal of award of damages for trademark infringement.

FACT SUMMARY: A court ordered Cawy Bottling Co. (D), which had infringed on a trademark held by Maltina Corp. (P), to account for its profits, even though it did not divert any significant sales from Maltina (P).

CONCISE RULE OF LAW: One who infringes on another's trademark may be held to account for his profits, even if he did not divert sales from the mark holder.

FACTS: Blanco-Herrera (P) operated a Cuban corporation which produced a drink similar to nonalcoholic beer, called "Malta Cristal" and "Cristal." He held Cuban and American trademarks. After the Cuban revolution, the communists confiscated his company, and he fled to the United States, where he formed Maltina Corporation (P) and assigned his U.S. trademark to the Corporation (P). While the beverages had been popular in the United States prior to the Cuban revolution, Maltina (P) was never able to raise sufficient capital to commence operations in the United States. Meanwhile, Cawy Bottling Co. (D) began distributing Malta under the name "Cristal," using a label that resembled the one formerly employed by Blanco-Herrera's (P) company. He sued for trademark infringement. A district court awarded an injunction and ordered an accounting. Cawy (D) appealed the accounting portion of the award.

ISSUE: May one who infringes on another's trademark be held to account for his profits even if he did not divert sales from the mark holder?

HOLDING AND DECISION: (Johnson, J.) Yes. One who infringes on another's trademark may be held to account for his profits, even if he did not divert sales from the mark holder. Courts are split as to whether to measure infringement damages as compensation for lost sales or as unjust enrichment. This court is of the opinion that the latter measure is the more appropriate. First, to force an infringer to account for profits even in the absence of actual sales diversions from the mark holder would further Congress' purpose in enacting trademark law, which was to make infringement unprofitable. Second, the holder of the mark has a property interest in the mark, and use of the mark violates that interest, even if no sales were diverted. For these reasons, proof of sales diversions is unnecessary for an infringer to be compelled to account for his profits. Here, since Cawy (D) definitely infringed it was proper to hold it to account. Affirmed.

EDITOR'S ANALYSIS: The types of remedies afforded in an infringement action usually depend on the culpability of the defendant. A successful plaintiff is usually afforded an injunction at the very least. Whether or not he can obtain an order awarding damages usually depends on whether the defendant was aware of its infringement. Here, Cawy (D) had been aware.

NOTES:

PIKLE-RITE CO. v. CHICAGO PICKLE CO.

171 F. Supp. 671, 121 U.S.P.Q. 128 (N.D. Ill. 1959).

NATURE OF CASE: Action for injunction and damages for trademark infringement.

FACT SUMMARY: Pikle-Rite Co. (P) brought an infringement action against the maker of a similarly-named pickle product, even though a visual comparison of the labels revealed no similarity.

CONCISE RULE OF LAW: A similarly-named product may infringe on a trademark even if a visual comparison of the labels would tend to reveal no similarity.

FACTS: Pickle-Rite Co. (P) produced several types of pickle products, which it sold under the name "Polka," along with a representation of a dancing couple. The label and name were trademarked. Subsequent to this, Chicago Pickle Co. (D) began marketing a pickle product called "Pol-Pak," referring to the Polish origin of the pickles. Pikle-Rite (P) sued for infringement, seeking an injunction and damages. Chicago (D) denied infringement in that the labels were dissimilar.

ISSUE: May a similarly-named product infringe on a trademark even if a visual comparison of the labels would tend to reveal no similarity?

HOLDING AND DECISION: (Hoffman, J.) Yes. A similarly-named product may infringe on a trademark even if a visual comparison of the labels would tend to reveal no similarity. The main issue in a trademark infringement action is whether the public is likely to be confused between the products at issue. While visual representations can be important, the names of products are the ultimate identifiers thereof. Further, shoppers do not always get to perform side-by-side comparisons of products' labels. For this reason, the purchasing public's likelihood of confusion is to be gauged from the presentation of similarly-named products singly, not side-by-side. Here, the names "Polka" and "Pol-Pak" are sufficiently similar that the purchasing public is likely to become confused between the two, despite the dissimilarity of labels. [The court went on to grant an injunction but denied damages on account of the lack of bad faith on the part of Chicago Pickle Co. (D).]

EDITOR'S ANALYSIS: Any trademark will be made up of different features. Some will be more important and/or distinctive than others. Here, a significant similarity was the first syllable of the product name. Nonetheless, since the beginning of a name is often the part most remembered, this was sufficient to constitute infringement. In addition, all the letters in the five-letter name "Polka" were contained in the infringing six-letter "Pol-Pak" name, with the one additional letter in the latter being the "P," the first letter in "Polka." A quick glance at the names could cause a harried shopper to miss the product distinction.

NOTES:

McGREGOR-DONIGER, INC. v.. DRIZZLE, INC.

599 F.2d 1126, 202 U.S.P.Q. 81 (2d Cir. 1979).

NATURE OF CASE: Appeal of dismissal of trademark infringement action.

FACT SUMMARY: A district court dismissed McGregor-Doniger's (P) infringement action against Drizzle, Inc. (D) on the basis that no likelihood of confusion existed between their noncompeting products.

CONCISE RULE OF LAW: With respect to noncompeting products, trademark infringement will not occur if no likelihood of confusion between the products exists.

NOTES:

FACTS: McGregor-Doniger, Inc. (P) produced an inexpensive golf jacket which it called "Drizzle." Subsequent to this, Drizzle, Inc. (D) began marketing a fashionable women's raincoat which it called "Drizzle." McGregor-Doniger (P) filed an action for trademark infringement. The district court, after a bench trial, found the products to be noncompeting, and that no likelihood of confusion between the products existed. It dismissed the action, and McGregor (P) appealed.

ISSUE: Will trademark infringement occur, with respect to non-competing products, if no likelihood of confusion between the products exists?

HOLDING AND DECISION: (Meskill, J.) No. With respect to non-competing products, trademark infringement will not occur if no likelihood of confusion between the products exists. When dissimilar products have the same or similar marks, an infringement occurs only if the public is likely to become confused by the products. Here, the district court held the products different, and this conclusion is supported. Likelihood of confusion requires an analysis of numerous factors. These include distinctiveness of the mark, similarity of the marks, product proximity, quality of defendant's product, whether the plaintiff is likely to enter the defendant's market, evidence of actual confusion, the defendant's good faith, and the sophistication of buyers. Here, the district court erred in requiring the plaintiff's mark to have acquired a secondary meaning to be called distinctive, but this does not alter the final result. While the marks are substantially the same, the district court found (1) the products were not sold in proximity to each other; (2) the qualities of the products differed, with Drizzle's (D) quality higher; (3) McGregor (P) was unlikely to enter Drizzle's (D) market; (4) no evidence of actual confusion existed; (5) no intentional infringement by Drizzle occurred; and (6) relative buyer sophistication was sufficient to discern a clear difference. These conclusions support the trial court's finding of no likelihood of confusion, so its judgment was proper. Affirmed.

EDITOR'S ANALYSIS: Distinctiveness of a mark is also known as "strength" of a mark. This refers to how strongly it identifies a particular product with a particular manufacturer. The potential for distinctiveness varies with the category of the mark. A generic mark cannot be distinctive; an arbitrary or fanciful mark can hardly be anything but distinctive. Here, the word "drizzle" fell into a category that could be called "descriptive," which falls between the aforementioned poles of the distinctiveness continuum.

CAN-AM ENGINEERING CO. v. HENDERSON GLASS, INC.

814 F.2d 253, 2 U.S.P.Q.2d 1197 (6th Cir. 1987).

NATURE OF CASE: Appeal of dismissal of action for damages for violation of § 43 of the Lanham Act.

FACT SUMMARY: Henderson Glass (D) used a depiction of a product made by Can-Am (P) in an advertisement in place of a more established similar product.

CONCISE RULE OF LAW: One does not violate § 43 of the Lanham Act if he does not attempt to misappropriate the goodwill of another product.

FACTS: Henderson Glass, Inc. (D) wished to advertise GM wire wheel covers that it sold. It made up flyers depicting a wire wheel cover, to be distributed to potential bulk purchasers. Henderson (D) had no photo of such a wheel cover in its files, so it took a photo of a wire wheel cover manufactured by Can-Am Engineering Co. (P), a new entrant into the field, and superimposed "GM" over Can-Am's (P) logo. Nonetheless, the distinctive geometric shape of Can-Am's (P) logo was evident. Upon Can-Am's (P) protest, Henderson (D) mailed an explanatory letter to its buyers and agreed to a consent order not to repeat the situation. Can-Am (P) then sued for damages under § 43 of the Lanham Act, alleging false designation of origin. The district court dismissed, and Can-Am (P) appealed.

ISSUE: Does one violate § 43 of the Lanham Act if he does not attempt to misappropriate the goodwill of another product?

HOLDING AND DECISION: (Guy, J.) No. One does not violate § 43 of the Lanham Act if one does not attempt to misappropriate the goodwill of another product. Section 43 of the Lanham Act provides for damages if a party attempts to affix a false designation or representation of the origin of a product. This section is analogous to common law unfair competition. For an aggrieved party to actually have been damaged, it is necessary that the false designator have misappropriated the goodwill of the misdesignated product. If this is not done, no damage has occurred. Here, Henderson (D) misrepresented Can-Am's (P) product, which was new and without an established market, as a GM product, which had an established market. If anything, this would create public confusion benefiting Can-Am (P), not damaging it. For this reason, its complaint was properly dismissed. Affirmed.

EDITOR'S ANALYSIS: The classic case of a § 43 violation is illustrated in the case L'Aiglon Apparel, Inc. v. Lana Lobell, Inc., 214 F.2d 649 (3d Cir. 1954). There, a maker of a cheap imitation dress published a photo of the superior original dress in its advertisements, a case of "palming off." The main case did not present this situation, as palming off was not engaged in by any means.

NOTES:

JOHNSON & JOHNSON v. CARTER-WALLACE, INC.

631 F.2d 186, 208 U.S.P.Q. 169 (2d Cir. 1980).

NATURE OF CASE: Appeal of dismissal of action alleging violations of the Lanham Act.

FACT SUMMARY: An equitable action under § 43 of the Lanham Act was dismissed due to Johnson & Johnson's (P) failure to produce evidence that the allegedly false advertising had diminished its sales.

CONCISE RULE OF LAW: For an injunction to issue under § 43 of the Lanham Act, a plaintiff need not show an actual loss in sales.

FACTS: Johnson & Johnson (P) marketed a product known as baby oil, a product which it advertised as an adjunct to shaving. Subsequent to this, Carter-Wallace, Inc. (D) began advertising a depilatory product, "Nair," which it claimed contained baby oil. Johnson & Johnson (P) brought an action under § 43 of the Lanham Act, alleging a false description and/or representation of "Nair" by Carter-Wallace (D). At trial, Johnson (P) did not produce evidence of a diminution in sales. The trial court granted a nonsuit dismissing the action, and Johnson (P) appealed.

ISSUE: Must a plaintiff show an actual loss in sales for an injunction to issue under § 43 of the Lanham Act?

HOLDING AND DECISION: (Mansfield, J.) No. For an injunction to issue under § 43 of the Lanham Act a plaintiff need not show an actual loss in sales. At common law, a false advertising action required such proof, which is extremely difficult to produce in an open market. However, pursuant to § 43's purpose of securing a marketplace free from deceitful marketing practices, § 43 was enacted without a requirement that actual loss be shown. All that is required is that a plaintiff have a reasonable belief that the alleged false advertiser's marketing practice negatively affects its sales. Here, both baby oil and Nair relate to hair removal. It therefore stands to reason that additions to Nair's market will result in a loss to baby oil's market. Consequently, Johnson & Johnson (P) met its evidentiary burden on this issue. The matter must therefore be remanded to the district court for a determination on the issue whether Carter-Wallace's (D) advertising was in fact deceptive. Reversed.

EDITOR'S ANALYSIS: Section 43 affords both injunctive relief and damages. The change in common law rule noted by the court only applied to request for injunctions. If a plaintiff wants to obtain damages, it still has to prove actual market losses, a difficult thing to show.

NOTES:

GRAHAM v. JOHN DEERE CO.

383 U.S. 1 (1966).

NATURE OF CASE: Review of denial of patent application.

FACT SUMMARY: Graham (P) submitted for a patent a plow accessory that was an extension of the state-of-the-art design.

CONCISE RULE OF LAW: A device which is an extension of the state of the art for that type of device is not patentable.

FACTS: Graham (P) submitted for patenting a plow chisel that, because of its flexible nature, supposedly had certain advantages when used in certain types of soil. The Patent Office denied the patent application, finding the design a mere extension of the state of the art, and an obvious improvement on existing technology. The court of appeals affirmed, and the Supreme Court granted review.

ISSUE: Is a device which is an extension of the state of the art for that type of device patentable?

HOLDING AND DECISION: (Clark, J.) No. A device which is an extension of the state of art for that type of device is not patentable. Section 103 of the Patent Act, enacted in 1952, mandates nonpatentability in the case of designs which would be obvious to a person having ordinary skill in the field related to the design in question. This section appears to be a codification of the longstanding judicial requirement that a device, to be patentable, must be the result of something more than the ordinary skill found in the field. Rather, a higher level of ingenuity is required. The work, in short, must be the product of an inventor, not a skillful mechanic. Here, the Patent Office found that the chisel in question did not represent a leap forward in design technology but rather was a logical improvement in design which could have been designed by anyone skilled in the field. This finding, not clearly erroneous, leads to the result that, under § 103 of the Patent Act, the chisel was not patentable. Affirmed.

EDITOR'S ANALYSIS: The enactment of § 103 constituted the first statutory addition of an element of patentability since the beginning of the republic. The 1790 Patent Act instituted the dual requirements of novelty and utility. These two requirements remained the cornerstones of patent law until the addition of § 103. Arguments were made that § 103 was an attempt to relax the judicially-imposed requirement of greater-than-ordinary skill in a device's creation, but the Court held the section to be a codification of the rule.

NOTES:

APPLICATION OF BORST

U.S.C.C.P.A., 52 C.C.P.A. 1398 (1965).

NOTES:

NATURE OF CASE: Appeal of denial of patent application.

FACT SUMMARY: Borst's patent application for a method of containing neutron radiation during a nuclear reaction was rejected on the grounds that an unpublished manuscript had evidenced prior knowledge of the system.

CONCISE RULE OF LAW: A patent application will not be rejected solely on the basis that an unpublished manuscript had reflected the idea behind the product for which a patent is sought.

FACTS: Borst applied for a patent on a system he had designed for containing neutron radiation during nuclear reactions. However, the Patent Office rejected the application on the basis of prior knowledge. This was predicated on the existence of a classified memorandum in which a system such as that designed by Borst was discussed, purely on a conceptual level. Borst appealed.

ISSUE: Will a patent application be rejected solely on the basis that an unpublished manuscript had reflected the idea behind the product for which a patent is sought?

HOLDING AND DECISION: (Smith, J.) No. A patent application will not be rejected solely on the basis that an unpublished manuscript had reflected the idea behind the product for which a patent is sought. Under 35 U.S.C. § 102(a), for a patent to issue, the thing for which a patent is sought must not be previously known. However, for the previous knowledge sufficient to defeat a patent application to exist, that knowledge must be public, not secret. An unpublished or classified manuscript will not result in the type of public knowledge that will defeat a patent application. Here, the manuscript involved was in fact classified. [The court went on to note that § 155 of the Atomic Energy Act of 1954 mandated an exception to this rule with respect to patent applications related to atomic energy, and therefore affirmed the denial of the application.]

EDITOR'S ANALYSIS: A further requirement of prior knowledge is that the knowledge cannot be conceptual only, but must be reduced to practice. In this instance, the court seemed to ignore this requirement. It is not clear from the opinion whether this requirement did not apply due to some mandate of the Atomic Energy Act.

UMC ELECTRONICS v. UNITED STATES

816 F.2d 647 (Fed. Cir. 1988).

NOTES:

NATURE OF CASE: Appeal of dismissal of action for damages for unauthorized patent use.

FACT SUMMARY: UMC Electronics (P) had offered for sale to the Navy a product substantially the same as a product it attempted to patent more than one year later.

CONCISE RULE OF LAW: For purposes of the one-year prior sale bar to a patent, reduction to practice of the claimed invention at the time of sale is not an absolute requirement.

FACTS: The Navy had expressed dissatisfaction with certain acceleration measuring devices (ACAs) it incorporated in its airplanes. Aware of the dissatisfaction, UMC Electronics (P) contracted with the Navy to supply about 1,600 of yet-undeveloped improved units. UMC's (P) first attempted design proved insufficient to suit the Navy's needs. An altered design was later produced, which was patented. The Navy never purchased any of the units eventually developed, but rather issued specifications which incorporated features of UMC's ACA, which were eventually purchased from a competitor of UMC (P). The patent application had been made over one year after the first units had been offered to the Navy. UMC (P) sued the federal Government (D) for unauthorized use of its patent. The district court dismissed, and UMC (P) appealed.

ISSUE: For purposes of the one-year prior sale bar to a patent, is reduction to practice of the claimed invention at the time of sale an absolute requirement?

HOLDING AND DECISION: (Nies, J.) No. For purposes of the one-year prior sale bar to a patent, reduction to practice of the claimed invention at the time of sale is not an absolute requirement. Section 102(b) of the Patent Act bars from patentability any product that has been offered for sale more than one year prior to the date of application for the patent. Here, the first edition of UMC's (P) ACA had been offered for sale more than one year prior to its patent application for the second model. The issue thus arises as to whether the unit put up for sale must exactly mirror the product for which application is made; in other words, had the applied-for product been reduced to practice? Case law is not uniform. Some authority requires such reduction, others require only an offer to sell within more than a year. This court believes that the purpose behind § 102(b), which is to compel an inventor to patent his product at an early date, is better served if the year statute is considered to have begun running when a product is offered for sale. Here, such offer was made more than one year prior to the application, so the patent was invalid, and the action was properly dismissed. Affirmed.

EDITOR'S ANALYSIS: Another issue which can arise in the context of the § 102(b) bar is the type of sale involved. Any general offering to the public or some segment thereof will constitute a sale. However, a single exchange for research purposes will not. Between these two ends of the spectrum any number of sales situations is possible, and holdings in this area are of necessity very case-specific.

PAULIK v. RIZKALLA

760 F.2d 1270, 226 U.S.P.Q. 224 (Fed. Cir. 1985).

NOTES:

NATURE OF CASE: Appeal of order awarding priority of invention.

FACT SUMMARY: Paulik's (P) having had a long period of inactivity prior to resuming work on a process was held to be a forfeiture of priority.

CONCISE RULE OF LAW: A period of inactivity in working on an invention will not by itself result in a forfeiture of priority.

FACTS: Paulik (P) reduced to practice a certain chemical process in 1970. He ceased work on it, attempting to find a corporate assignee to exploit the process. In January 1975, Paulik (P) recommenced work on the process. In March 1975, Rizkalla (D) having independently formulated the process, applied for a patent. In June 1975, Paulik (P) applied therefor. Paulik (P) then filed an action seeking a determination of priority. The U.S. Patent and Trademark Office Board held Paulik's (P) period of inactivity on the process to have constituted a waiver of priority, and declared Rizkalla (D) the senior party. Paulik (P) appealed.

ISSUE: Will a period of inactivity in working on an invention by itself result in a forfeiture of priority?

HOLDING AND DECISION: (Newman, J.) No. A period of inactivity in working on an invention will not in itself result in a forfeiture of priority. Section 102(g) provides that a party abandoning or concealing an invention shall not be entitled to patent priority as against one who has not done so. A decision based on § 102(g) must take into account dates of conception, reduction, and all relevant equities. The Board in this instance apparently was of the opinion that any abandonment per se constitutes a forfeiture. This court disagrees with that conclusion. Reasons, economic or otherwise, may necessitate suspension of research for a period of time. To hold that one so abandoning may lose his priority would discourage inventors from following up on inventions, a result not in the national interest. Consequently, any period of inactivity must be viewed in light of all relevant circumstances. Here, Paulik (P) reduced the process at issue to practice in 1970, and put it aside for legitimate economic reasons. He then recommenced work on it prior to Rizkalla's (D) reduction to practice. In view of these facts, Paulik (P) should not be held to have forfeited priority. Reversed.

EDITOR'S ANALYSIS: Patent priority is not a race to the Patent Office. Rules for priority of perfecting an invention operate with respect to patent seniority, not priority of filing. However, as noted by the court in this opinion, one perfecting an invention cannot sit on it too long, on pain of being subjected to § 102(g).

HAZELTINE RESEARCH, INC. v. BRENNER

382 U.S. 252 (1965).

NATURE OF CASE: Appeal of dismissal of action to compel issuance patent.

FACT SUMMARY: Regis (P) was denied a patent on the basis that a prior pending application constituted a prior art sufficient to render Regis' (P) product not new for purposes of patentability.

CONCISE RULE OF LAW: For purposes of the newness requirement, the technology contained in a pending application may constitute prior art.

FACTS: Regis (P) applied for a patent on a microwave switch he had developed. The Patent Office denied the application, citing one Wallace's prior application not granted at the time of Regis' (P) application. The Office concluded that the state of the art embodied in Wallace's application was such as to render Regis' (P) design insufficiently novel for patenting purposes. Regis (P) appealed, contending that a pending application should not be considered in assessing prior state of the art. The Board of Appeals affirmed. A district court dismissed Regis' (P) subsequent action to compel issuance of a patent, and the court of appeals affirmed. The Supreme Court granted review.

ISSUE: For purposes of the newness requirement, may the technology contained in a pending application constitute prior art?

HOLDING AND DECISION: (Black, J.) Yes. For purposes of the newness requirement, the technology contained in a pending application may constitute prior art. It has long been the rule that disclosures in a patent application become part of the prior art at the time of application, not approval. This has been based on the notion that patentability should not turn on the vagarities of the Patent Office's backlog. Nothing in the 1952 Patent Act reversed this rule, so it remains in effect. Here, the Patent Office decided that Wallace's prior application occupied the state of the art prior to Regis' (P), and his patent application was therefore properly denied. Affirmed.

EDITOR'S ANALYSIS: The approach urged by Regis (P) in this case would have greatly lessened standards of patentability. The Patent Office's backlog of pending applications is usually quite lengthy. To disallow pending application from constituting prior art would have resulted in many patents issued on inventions lacking true novelty, a result no doubt contrary to legislative intent in this area.

NOTES:

BRENNER v. MANSON

383 U.S. 519 (1966).

NATURE OF CASE: Review of order reversing denial of patent application.

FACT SUMMARY: Manson (P) sought to patent a chemical process whose only demonstrable utility was to aid in research.

CONCISE RULE OF LAW: A process whose only demonstrable utility is to aid in research is not patentable.

FACTS: Manson (P) sought to patent a chemical process for synthesizing certain steroidal compounds. Although these compounds were not in themselves beneficial, they were useful in cancer research. The Patent Office denied the application on the basis that the process was not useful. The Court of Customs and Patent Appeals reversed, and the Supreme Court granted review.

ISSUE: Is a process whose only demonstrable utility is to aid in research patentable?

HOLDING AND DECISION: (Fortas, J.) No. A process whose only demonstrable utility is to aid in research is not patentable. It has been the rule since the inception of patent law that, for an invention to be patentable, it must be useful. An invention must not only be harmless, it must also not be frivolous or insignificant. The question thus presents itself as to whether a product or process is useful if, rather than being useful in itself, it is the subject of serious scientific inquiry. While the Patent Act is silent on this issue, an examination of the purposes of the patent law reveals that the answer must be in the negative. The basis quid pro quo of patent law is that a monopoly is granted in exchange for a finished thing with substantial utility. A product or process useful as the subject of research does not fit this requirement. Further, to allow a monopoly on the research stage of innovation might well inhibit such innovation, in direct contravention to the purposes of patent law. Here, the process in question is capable only of synthesizing products suitable for research, not useful in themselves. The process is therefore not patentable. Reversed.

DISSENT: (Harlan, J.) The Court's policy arguments against the patentability of processes which are useful in generating objects of study are not convincing. Further, decisional history tends to support such patentability.

EDITOR'S ANALYSIS: Utility is one of the basic requirements of patent law. Indeed, it is one of the characteristics relating to patents described in Art. I, § 8 of the Constitution. Congress, in its first Patent Act (enacted in 1790), mandated this requirement. It is now codified at 35 U.S.C. § 101.

NOTES:

W.L. GORE & ASSOCIATES v. GARLOCK, INC.

721 F.2d 1540, 220 U.S.P.Q. 303 (Fed. Cir. 1983).

NATURE OF CASE: Appeal of order invalidating patents.

FACT SUMMARY: Two patents were invalidated on the basis of post-application developments in the state of the art which rendered certain portions of the application indefinite.

CONCISE RULE OF LAW: Post-application developments in the state of the art which render a patent application indefinite do not invalidate a patent issued thereon.

FACTS: W.L. Gore & Associates (P) obtained patents on a pair of processes involving polymers. Both applications used the phrase "stretching time," which at the time of application was accepted in the polymer field to mean percentage of unit length stretched divided by time spent stretching. Subsequent to the application, the term became more ambiguous in the field. Subsequently, W.L. Gore & Associates (P) sued Garlock, Inc. (D) for infringement. A district court held the patents invalid on the basis that ambiguity as to the meaning of "stretch rate" made the applications insufficient. W.L. Gore (P) appealed.

ISSUE: Do post-application developments in the state of the art which render a patent application indefinite invalidate a patent issued thereon?

HOLDING AND DECISION: (Markey, J.) No. Post-application developments in the state of the art which render a patent application indefinite do not invalidate a patent issued thereon. Section 112 of the Patent Act requires that a patent application be sufficiently specific so as to enable one of ordinary skill in the field to reproduce the matter for which the patent is sought. The state of the art prevalent to this issue is that existing at the time of the application; post-application developments may not be used to retroactively invalidate a patent. Here, "stretching time" had a definite meaning at the time of patent application. Consequently, the subsequent development of ambiguity in the field as to the meaning of the term did not operate to invalidate the patent for being indefinite. Reversed.

EDITOR'S ANALYSIS: That an application must be definite is part of the enabling requirement of § 112. This requirement is part of the quid pro quo which forms the basis of patent law. The monopoly is granted to the inventor only on the condition that others may use the matter patented upon expiration of the patent. This is made possible partly through the enabling requirement.

NOTES:

DIAMOND v. CHAKRABARTY

447 U.S. 303 (1980).

NATURE OF CASE: Appeal of order reversing denial of patent application.

FACT SUMMARY: Chakrabarty (P) sought to patent a live, man-made microorganism.

CONCISE RULE OF LAW: A live, man-made microorganism may be patented.

FACTS: Chakrabarty (P) developed, through recombinant DNA processes, a new species of bacterium capable of metabolizing hydrocarbons in a manner unknown in naturally-occurring organisms. The microorganisms showed great promise in the treatment of oil spills. Chakrabarty (P) applied for a patent. The Patent Office denied the application on the basis that the microorganisms were unpatentable products of nature. The Board of Appeals affirmed. The Court of Customs and Patent Appeals reversed, and the Supreme Court granted review.

ISSUE: May a live, man-made microorganism be patented?

HOLDING AND DECISION: (Burger, C.J.) Yes. A live, man-made microorganism may be patented. Resolution of this issue is, despite its philosophical implications, strictly a matter of statutory construction. The relevant statute here, 35 U.S.C. § 101, defines as patentable any new and useful "manufacture" or "composition of matter," among other things. It is a basic rule of construction that words are given their natural, ordinary meanings. There can be little doubt that microorganisms produced by recombinant DNA technology may be said to be manufactured and to be compositions of matter. The fact they are alive is irrelevant for purposes of patent law. While it is true that naturally-occurring products may not be patented, a genetically-engineered microorganism is not naturally occurring. While this Court recognizes that recombinant DNA technology is a controversial field, it is ill-equipped to balance the competing values and interests manifested therein; this is Congress' task. Since the patent laws clearly include materials such as are at issue here within their ambit, and no specific law exists excluding it, the only appropriate holding is that recombinant DNA-produced microorganisms are patentable. Affirmed.

DISSENT: (Brennan, J.) Congress, in enacting the Plant Patent Act in 1930 and the Plant Variety Protection Act expressly exclude bacteria from patentability.

EDITOR'S ANALYSIS: The general rule is that things occurring naturally in the universe may not be patented. A type of plant occurring naturally could not be patented; neither could a natural principle. The laws of motion could not have been patented by Newton. This legal principle appears straightforward, but as the instant case demonstrates, modern science has made it less so.

NOTES:

YODER BROS., INC. v. CALIFORNIA-FLORIDA PLANT CORP.
537 F.2d 1347, 193 U.S.P.Q. 264 (5th Cir. 1977).

NATURE OF CASE: Appeal of award of damages for plant patent infringement.

FACT SUMMARY: California-Florida Plant Corporation (D) argued that Yoder Bros. (P) could not patent a strain of flower that genetically recurs frequently.

CONCISE RULE OF LAW: A strain of flower that genetically recurs frequently may be patented.

FACTS: Yoder Brothers, Inc. (P), through breeding of chrysanthemums, developed several distinctive strains which it patented pursuant to the 1930 Plant Patent Protection Act. Yoder (P) subsequently sued California-Florida Plant Corp. (D) for infringement of the patents. At trial, California-Florida (D) was not permitted to introduce evidence that the mutations from which the patented strains were derived recurred frequently in the species. The court held California-Florida (D) to have infringed, and it appealed.

ISSUE: May a strain of flower that genetically recurs frequently be patented?

HOLDING AND DECISION: (Goldberg, J.) Yes. A strain of flower that genetically recurs frequently may be patented. The 1930 Plant Patent Protection Act was passed largely to ensure that asexually produced plant varieties will be given the same patentability as are other types of inventions. For patentability, an invention must be useful, new, and nonobvious. In the context of plants, this means that a plant strain, to be patentable, must have some demonstrably desirable characteristic, be a strain actually engineered and not found naturally, and be the subject of invention. The issue presents itself as to whether a strain which meets these requirements can be patented if the strain is based on mutation that is shown to recur frequently, as the argument can be made that such a plant is not truly an invention. This court is of the opinion that such strains are in fact patentable. To hold that only strains representing a fundamental change in the biology of a plant are patentable would be to make plant patents more difficult to obtain than patents generally, as such a rigid requirement is not found generally. Since the purpose of the 1930 Act was to make patent laws of general application equally applicable to plant strains, the conclusion must be that a strain may be based on a common mutation will not deny patentability. This was the holding of the court below. Affirmed.

EDITOR'S ANALYSIS: The 1930 Act protects only asexually reproduced plants, which are produced by grafting. This limitation provided no incentive for private plant breeding programs. To stimulate research and commercial exploitation in this area, Congress in 1970 passed the Plant Variety Protection Act. This law made most aspects of patent law applicable to sexually reproduced varieties.

NOTES:

CALMAR, INC. v. COOK CHEMICAL COMPANY

383 U.S. 1 (1966).

NATURE OF CASE: Review of order dismissing challenge to patent validity.

FACT SUMMARY: Cook Chemical Company (P) contended that the commercial success of a spray container it developed militated in favor of patentability.

CONCISE RULE OF LAW: The fact that a product is commercially successful will not in itself make it patentable.

FACTS: Cook Chemical Company (P) developed a spray pump which was designed to be used in connection with insecticide sprays. The design differed minimally from prior efforts by other manufacturers. The only differences were certain aspects on top of the unit, and these differences were not significant. Nonetheless a patent was issued. Cook Chemical Co. (P) eventually brought an infringement suit against Calmar, Inc. (D). Calmar (D) contested the validity of the patent, showing the minor differences between Cook's (P) products and other patents. Cook (P) relied largely on the products' commercial success in arguing that the product was novel and not obvious. The court of appeals upheld the patent, and the Supreme Court granted review.

ISSUE: Will the fact that a product is commercially successful in itself make a product patentable?

HOLDING AND DECISION: (Clark, J.) No. The fact that a product is commercially successful in itself will not make a product patentable. To be patentable, a product must be both novel and nonobvious. While a product's commercial success may suggest these elements, these are factors which may be characterized as economic and motivational. Patentability is a technical issue. The thing for which a patent is sought must be sufficiently different from existent products that it would not be obvious to one versed in the state of the art. Here, the evidence plainly showed that Cook's (P) sprayer largely borrowed from existing knowledge, differing only in minor aspects relating to its cap design. It appears clear that the distinctions between the Cook (P) product and prior art were such as would be obvious. Therefore, the patent was invalid. Reversed.

EDITOR'S ANALYSIS: It is possible for a patent to issue for a product which, while not containing any new aspect, integrates them in a novel way. It is however, difficult to do. Such an applicant must face the obviousness bar of § 103 of the Patent Act. Often, a product composed of old technology will appear obvious in hindsight, even if it was not obvious in its inception.

NOTES:

PAPER CONVERTING MACHINE COMPANY v. MAGNA-GRAPHICS CORP.

745 F.2d 11, 223 U.S.P.Q. 591 (Fed. Cir. 1984).

NATURE OF CASE: Appeal of award of damages for patent infringement.

NOTES:

FACT SUMMARY: Magna-Graphics (D) partly assembled a product upon which Paper Converting Machine Co. (P) had a patent, although it did not complete the product until after the patent expired.

CONCISE RULE OF LAW: One infringes a patent if he begins manufacture of a patented product during the life of the patent, even if he does not complete it until after the patent's expiration.

FACTS: Paper Converting Machine Co. (P) obtained a patent on a paper-rolling machine. Near the end of the life of the patent, Magna-Graphics Corp. (D) contracted with a third party to deliver a similar device. The machine was built and delivered to the third party in a slightly uncompleted stage. After the patent expired, the machine was completed. Paper Converting (P) sued for infringement. A district court held infringement to have occurred and awarded damages. Magna-Graphics (D) appealed.

ISSUE: Does one infringe a patent if he begins manufacture of a patented product during the life of the patent even if he does not complete it until after the patent's expiration?

HOLDING AND DECISION: (Nichols, J.) Yes. One infringes a patent if he begins manufacture of a patented product during the life of the patent, even if he does not complete it until after the patent's expiration. Patent law gives the holder of a patent the right to exclude others from making, using, or selling a patented product during the life of the patent. The question thus arises as to whether "making" refers only to completing a product, or any process short of actual completion. Congress did not define the term. However, it seems clear to this court that the interpretation urged by Magna-Graphics (D), that "making" only refers to actual completion, was not within Congress' intent. To hold otherwise would make the last year or so of the statutory 17-year patent life meaningless, as a rival manufacturer could initiate mass production during the life of the patent and stop just short of completion, only completing when the patent expires. As this would lessen the protection afforded by the 17-year patent life, this court concludes that "making" means any fabrication, not just completion. This was the holding of the district court, and it was proper. Affirmed.

DISSENT: (Nies, J.) The Supreme Court in Deepsouth Packing Co. v. Laitram Corp., 406 U.S. 518 (1972), mandated a contrary result.

EDITOR'S ANALYSIS: Deepsouth involved a machine partially manufactured prior to the expiration of a related patent. The majority opinion disagreed with the dissent's view that Deepsouth applied. Deepsouth involved an extraterritorial product; U.S. patent laws do not have extraterritorial effect.

WILBUR-ELLIS COMPANY v. KUTHER

377 U.S. 422 (1964).

NATURE OF CASE: Review of award of damages for patent infringement.

FACT SUMMARY: Leuschner (D) repaired worn-out parts on a machine patented by Kuther (P) , replacing them with parts altering its function.

CONCISE RULE OF LAW: One does not infringe a patent when he replaces worn-out parts on a patented product with parts that alter its function.

FACTS: Kuther (P) had developed a machine which canned fish into one-pound cans. The machine was patented. One unit was sold to Wilbur-Ellis (D). Subsequently, certain parts wore out, and Leuschner (D) was hired to repair it. Per Wilbur-Ellis' (D) request, he used different parts to alter the machine's function so that it packed fish into five-ounce cans. Kuther (P) sued for infringement. A district court awarded damages, and the court of appeals affirmed. The Supreme Court granted certiorari.

ISSUE: Does one infringe a patent when he replaces worn-out parts on a patented product with parts that alter its function?

HOLDING AND DECISION: (Douglas, J.) No. One does not infringe a patent when he replaces worn-out parts on a patented product with parts that alter its function. It is not a patent infringement to repair a patented item. Further, the fact that the repair alters the function of the product is of no consequence. One having a patent on a product has a patent on the design only, not its use. When the patentee sells a machine or instrument whose sole value is in its use, he receives the consideration for its use and he parts with the right to restrict that use. Here, the work by Leuschner (D) was a legitimate repair, and the fact that the repair changed the product's use did not change that fact. Reversed.

EDITOR'S ANALYSIS: "Repair" does not infringe a patent; "reconstruction," however, does. This is based on the notion that reconstruction is a form of "making" and "making" is specifically included in the statutory language of patent law. Needless to say, the distinction between "repair" and "reconstruction" is an elusive one and has generated no small amount of litigation.

NOTES:

HANSON v. ALPINE VALLEY SKI AREA, INC.

718 F.2d 1075, 219 U.S.P.Q. 679 (Fed. Cir. 1983).

NATURE OF CASE: Appeal of award of damages for patent infringement.

FACT SUMMARY: Hanson (P) was awarded patent infringement damages based on reasonable royalty value of the patent.

CONCISE RULE OF LAW: Patent infringement damages may be measured as the reasonable royalty value of the patent.

FACTS: Hanson (P), in 1969, invented and patented a snowmaking process that was considerably more energy-efficient than the current technology. Subsequent to this, he sued Alpine Valley Ski Area, Inc. (D) for using duplicate machines. A district court found infringement. It awarded damages based on what it considered to be the reasonable royalty value of the patent, this measure being calculated as a percentage of expected savings to Alpine (D). Alpine (D) appealed.

ISSUE: May patent infringement damages be measured as the reasonable royalty value of the patent?

HOLDING AND DECISION: (Friedman, J.) Yes. Patent infringement damages may be measured as the reasonable royalty value of the patent. Damages in patent actions are governed by 35 U.S.C. § 284. This law provides that, if the evidence permits, actual damages will be the proper measure. However, if the record does not permit computation of this figure, the alternative measure will be the reasonable royalty value that the infringer would have been expected to pay in an arms-length transaction. This is a fact-intensive analysis, and is within the province of the district court to determine. Such a determination will be set aside only upon a clear showing of error. Here, the district court determined that an arms-length royalty agreement would have resulted in royalties being bases on a percentage of expected savings to Alpine (D). There is no showing that this was an erroneous conclusion, and it shall therefore be sustained. Affirmed.

CONCURRENCE: (Davis, J.) [Judge Davis' concurrence involved certain evidentiary matters not germane to the issue here.]

EDITOR'S ANALYSIS: The damages permitted by Congress in patent actions have changed over the years. Actual damages have always been an allowable measure. At one time, restitutionary damages were also permitted. This measure was dropped in 1946, when § 284 was enacted in substantially the form it exists today.

NOTES:

GRAVER TANK & MFG. CO. v. LINDE AIR PRODUCTS

329 U.S. 605 (1950).

NATURE OF CASE: Review of finding of patent infringement.

NOTES:

FACT SUMMARY: Linde Air Products (P) sued for patent infringement the maker of a welder that performed in a slightly different manner than did a welder upon which it had a patent.

CONCISE RULE OF LAW: A product which performs in a manner slightly different from a patented product may infringe that patent.

FACTS: Linde Air Products (P) obtained a patent on a welding device which used magnesium silicate in its process. Graver Tank & Manufacturing Company (D) developed a welding device which incorporated the same techniques embodied in the Linde (P) device, but which used manganese silicate instead of magnesium silicate. Linde (P) sued for patent infringement. The district court, finding the two devices to be the same except for the types of silicate used and this difference to be unimportant, held several patents valid and infringed. Several other patents were held invalid. The court of appeals partially reversed, holding all the patents valid and infringed. The Supreme Court granted certiorari.

ISSUE: May a product which performs in a manner slightly different from a patented product infringe that patent?

HOLDING AND DECISION: (Jackson, J.) Yes. A product which performs in a manner slightly different from a patented product may infringe that patent. If any variation on the design of a patented product would make the patent inapplicable, the value of a patent would be nil. Virtually any product or process can be varied slightly and perform in an identical fashion. For this reason, courts have developed the doctrine of equivalents. If a product or process performs substantially the same function in substantially the same way to obtain the same result as a patented product or process, the patent is infringed. Here, the district court found that the only difference between the two products was the type of silicate used, and that the difference was unimportant. This finding, not clearly erroneous, supports the holding of a patent infringement. Affirmed.

DISSENT: (Black, J.) A patent application must specify what contained in the application is new and the product of invention. Only these portions of the patented product may not be copied. The Court's decision today undercuts this rule, as it may lead to monopolization of non-novel aspects of a product.

DISSENT: (Douglas, J.) The specifications of a product may not be patented. The Court seems to be willing to patent a product's specifications and then apply the doctrine of equivalents to a product with a similar specification.

EDITOR'S ANALYSIS: The doctrine of equivalents was established in Winans v. Denmead, 56 U.S. 330 (1853). Despite its age, the doctrine is still not completely settled. Some courts take an element-by-element approach. Others tend to look at the product as a whole in applying the doctrine. The Supreme Court has never ruled on this issue.

TOWNSEND ENGINEERING CO. v. HITEC CO.

829 F.2d 1086, 4 U.S.P.Q.2d 1136 (Fed. Cir. 1987).

NATURE OF CASE: Appeal of summary judgment dismissing patent infringement action.

FACT SUMMARY: Townsend Engineering (P), having made certain amendments on a product to obtain a patent, contended that a similar product having no characteristics added by the amendments infringed on the patent.

CONCISE RULE OF LAW: A product having no characteristics added to a product to obtain a patent thereon does not infringe on that patent.

FACTS: Townsend Engineering Co. (P) designed a sausage rolling machine which it claimed to be an improvement over a model on which it already had a patent. The examiner denied the application, holding that the changes were obvious in relation to the prior patent. In response to this, Townsend (P) added certain features. A patent was issued. Subsequent to this, Townsend (P) sued Hitec Co. (D), maker of a competing product, for infringement. The district court held that the Hitec (D) device had no features similar to those added to the Townsend (P) device by the amendments and found no infringement. The court granted summary judgment, and Townsend (P) appealed.

ISSUE: Does a product having no characteristics similar to those added to a product to obtain a patent thereon infringe on that patent?

HOLDING AND DECISION: (Friedman, J.) No. A product having no characteristics similar to those added to a product to obtain a patent thereon does not infringe on that patent. A party seeking a patent may not make changes in a patent application to avoid running afoul of a statutory requirement for patent approval and then claim infringement by a product that has none of those new characteristics. While it is true that, under the doctrine of equivalents, an infringing product need not be an exact image of the patented product, one who has incorporated certain characteristics specifically to obtain a patent cannot claim infringement on a product without these characteristics. Here, the district court found that Townsend (P) did that very thing and properly dismissed. Affirmed.

EDITOR'S ANALYSIS: The rule involved by the court here is called prosecution history estoppel. It is based on the notion that a competitor, who is on notice of the prosecution history of a patent, should be able to rely on the fact that certain elements were essential to a patent and design a product which does not contain those elements. Interestingly, proof of reliance is not a condition precedent to involving the doctrine.

NOTES:

HASBRO BRADLEY, INC. v. SPARKLE TOYS, INC.

780 F.2d 189, 228 U.S.P.Q. 423 (2d Cir. 1985).

NATURE OF CASE: Appeal from grant of injunctive relief.

FACT SUMMARY: Sparkle (D) contended that Takara's failure to affix a copyright notice to toys distributed in Japan placed such toys' design in the public domain, allowing Sparkle (D) to legally copy them.

CONCISE RULE OF LAW: The omission of notice from copies of a protected work may be cured, preventing the work from entering the public domain.

FACTS: Takara, a Japanese toymaker, designed, manufactured and distributed robotic toys in Japan. The toys bore no copyright notice as required in the United States, but not required in Japan. Approximately 213,000 unmarked toys were distributed. Takara granted the U.S. copyright to Hasbro (P), which distributed duly marked toys in the United States. Sparkle (D) copied the design of the toys and began distributing such copies in the United States. Hasbro (P) successfully petitioned for a preliminary injunction to stop Sparkle (D) from infringing on its copyright. Sparkle (D) appealed, contending Takara's original failure to include a copyright notice placed the design in the public domain.

ISSUE: Can the omission of copyright notice from copies of a protected work be cured to prevent it from entering the public domain?

HOLDING AND DECISION: (Friendly, J.) Yes. The omission of copyright notice from copies of a protected work may be cured, preventing it from entering the public domain. Hasbro (P), as the copyright holder, had the ability to cure the omission. By adding the notice within five years of the original publication of the work, the omission was cured. Under § 405 of the Copyright Act of 1976, the work was then protected from the date of its first publication. Thus, Sparkle (D) violated the copyright, and the injunction was proper. Affirmed.

EDITOR'S ANALYSIS: The court rejected the proposition that an intentional omission of the copyright notice could not be cured. In this case, the notice was omitted because it was unnecessary in Japan. Thus, a question as to intent existed. Further, the court reserved the question of Hasbro's (P) responsibility to use efforts to mark the unmarked toys previously distributed.

NOTES:

BLEISTEIN v. DONALDSON LITHOGRAPHING CO.
188 U.S. 239 (1903).

NATURE OF CASE: Appeal from an affirmation of a decision for a directed verdict in a suit to recover penalties for copyright infringement.

FACT SUMMARY: Donaldson Lithographic Co. (D) copied in reduced form three chromolithographs Bleistein (P) had prepared for advertising Wallace's circus.

CONCISE RULE OF LAW: Chromolithographs are entitled to copyright protection even if designed for advertising purposes.

FACTS: In order to advertise his circus, Wallace hired Bleistein (P), who produced three chromolithographs depicting some of the acts to be seen therein, showing a picture of Wallace in the corner, and indicating the subject therein portrayed and the fact that the corresponding reality was to be seen at the circus. One chromolithograph utilized an ordinary ballet scene, another depicted the Stirk family performing on bicycles, and the third showed groups of men and women whitened to represent statues. When Donaldson Lithographic (D) subsequently produced reduced copies of these three advertisement chromolithographs, Bleistein (P) sued to recover penalties for copyright infringement. Arguing that chromolithographs were not entitled to protection under federal statutes allowing a copyright to the "author, designer, or proprietor ... of any engraving, cut, print ... (or) chromo," Donaldson (D) obtained a directed verdict that was upheld on appeal. On this further appeal, Donaldson (D) again asserts that chromolithographs do not meet the criteria for copyright protection in lieu of a provision in the act of 1874 that the words "engraving," "cut," and "print" shall be applied only to pictorial illustrations or works connected with the fine arts.

ISSUE: Are chromolithographs, designed for advertising purposes, barred from copyright protection?

HOLDING AND DECISION: (Holmes, J.) No. The fact that a chromolithograph was produced as an advertisement vehicle does not alter the fact that such "pictorial illustrations" are copyrightable. Even if the court were to hold that the act of 1874 limits the words "engraving," "cut," and "print" to pictorial illustrations connected with the fine arts or works connected with the fine arts (instead of viewing the qualifying phrase, "connected with the fine arts" as applicable only to the word "works"), this decision would not change. The antithesis to "illustrations or works connected with the fine arts" is not works of little merit or humble degree, or illustrations addressed to the less educated classes; it is "print or labels designed to be used for any other articles of manufacture." To hold otherwise would be to set up the judiciary as an arbiter of artistic quality. Some works of genius would be sure to miss appreciation because they spoke in a new language not yet appreciated. The fact that a picture might have broad appeal to a public less educated than the judge should not be a bar to protecting the work, whose public appreciation makes its value obvious. In this case, the very fact that there was a desire to reproduce the chromolithographs outside the advertisement framework shows that they had their worth. As protection should have been afforded, the judgment below is reversed.

DISSENT: (Harlan, J.) A pictorial illustration must have some intrinsic value other than its function as an advertisement to be copyrightable, as copyright protection is not offered to mere labels simply designating or describing an article. A connection with the fine arts is what gives this needed intrinsic value, but anything other than advertising value is lacking here.

EDITOR'S ANALYSIS: One point the dissenting justice completely overlooks is that, under previous decisions, the chromolithographs would have been copyrightable had they been designed for no purpose beyond artistic expression. Whatever artistic value was inherent then is hardly changed by the subsequent use.

NOTES:

MILLER v. UNIVERSAL CITY STUDIOS, INC.

65 F.2d 1365, 212 U.S.P.Q. 345 (5th Cir. 1981).

NATURE OF CASE: Appeal of award of damages for copyright infringement.

FACT SUMMARY: Miller (P) contended that the use of facts he had developed through research and used as the basis for a book he wrote was an infringement of his copyright.

CONCISE RULE OF LAW: The product of research cannot be copyrighted.

FACTS: Miller (P) write a book about an unsuccessful kidnapping that occurred during the 1970s. Universal City Studios, Inc. (D) approached Miller (P) about purchasing the rights to the book, but negotiations were never consummated. Nonetheless, Universal (P) produced a TV-movie about the event. Miller (P) sued Universal (D) and the screenwriter for copyright infringement. The district court instructed the jury that "research is copyrightable." The jury awarded $200,000, and an appeal was taken.

ISSUE: Can the product of research be copyrighted?

HOLDING AND DECISION: (Roney, J.) No. The product of research cannot be copyrighted. Ideas and facts are not copyrightable; only the expression thereof is. To the extent that expression is determined by the nature of the fact or idea involved, such expression is not copyrightable, either. Copyright law embodies the notion that facts are in the public domain. Once published, a fact can be used by anyone. Consequently, if a person adduces a set of facts by research and publishes the facts, the facts themselves cannot be copyrighted. Here, the court's instruction essentially told the jury that facts themselves could be copyrighted. This was contrary to copyright law. [The court went on to reject the argument that the error was harmless.] Reversed.

EDITOR'S ANALYSIS: The rule embodied here is fairly universal among the circuits. Examples of it are fairly common, particularly in the realm of historical research. Examples include Rosemont Enterprises v. Random House, 366 F.2d 303 (2d Cir. 1966), which involved facts regarding Howard Hughes, and Huehling v. Universal City Studios, 618 F.2d 972 (2d Cir. 1979).

NOTES:

DONALD v. ZACK MEYER'S T.V. SALES AND SERV.

426 F.2d 1027, 165 U.S.P.Q. 751 (5th Cir. 1970).

NATURE OF CASE: Appeal of order enjoining copyright infringement.

FACT SUMMARY: Donald (P) sought to copyright contractual language in which the substance in each part could be found in other sources.

CONCISE RULE OF LAW: Contractual language in which the substance of each part can be found in other sources is not copyrightable.

FACTS: Donald (P) submitted to the copyright office a preprinted contract involving chattel paper. Donald (P), a nonlawyer with some legal education, had obtained each relevant section of the agreement by using published legal forms, although he had arranged them into the order of his choosing. Subsequent to this, Moore Business Forms, Inc. (D), which happened across a preprinted form, copied it. Donald (P), upon discovering this, sued for infringement. A district court declined to award damages, but enjoined future use of the language in the form. Moore (D) appealed.

ISSUE: Is contractual language in which the substance of each part can be found in other sources copyrightable?

HOLDING AND DECISION: (Goldberg, J.) No. contractual language in which the substance of each part can be found in other sources is not copyrightable. For a literary work to be copyrightable, it must be original. The threshold for originality sufficient to allow for copyrightability is not high; indeed, it has been said that originality means little more than a prohibition against copying. Nonetheless, to surmount the originality hurdle, an author has to do something more with source material than effecting a trivial addition or variation. Something substantial must be added. When everything of substance is borrowed from other work and only minor change is made, the work is not copyrightable. Here, everything in the contract was obtained from published works. The order was Donald's (P) formulation, but the order of matters in the agreement was not particularly important. In light of this, the material in question was not copyrightable. Reversed.

EDITOR'S ANALYSIS: Patent and copyright law part company with respect to the originality requirement. Patent law requires genuine newness or novelty; copyright law does not. One may liberally borrow from prior sources. As long as the material is expressed in an original manner, originality is satisfied.

NOTES:

BAKER v. SELDEN

101 U.S. 99 (1879).

NATURE OF CASE: Appeal from award of damages for copyright infringement.

FACT SUMMARY: Baker (D) sold forms similar to those Selden (P) had in his copyrighted book setting forth his system of bookkeeping.

CONCISE RULE OF LAW: The protection afforded by a copyright on a book explaining an art or system extends only to the author's unique explanation thereof and does not preclude others from using the system or the forms necessarily incidental to such use.

FACTS: Selden (P) copyrighted a book in which he used an introductory essay explaining his system of bookkeeping followed by forms to put the system to use. He had arranged the columns and headings so that the entire operation of a day, week, or month was on a single page or on two pages facing each other. Baker (D) subsequently began selling forms with differently arranged columns and headings to achieve the same result. When Selden (P) successfully brought suit for copyright infringement, Baker (D) appealed. He argued that the forms were noncopyrightable.

ISSUE: Does a copyright on a book explaining an art or system preclude others from using the system or the forms incidental to such use?

HOLDING AND DECISION: (Bradley, J.) No. A copyright on a book explaining an art or system protects only the author's unique explanation thereof and does not preclude others from using the system or the forms incidental to such use. To find that a copyright protected against use of the system itself or the forms necessary to such use would be to grant patent-type protection without requiring a showing of novelty. Copyright is based on originality, not novelty, and protects the explanation and not the use of the system explained. Here, therefore, the copyright Selden (P) obtained could not give him the exclusive right to use the bookkeeping system or the forms necessary to such use. Reversed.

EDITOR'S ANALYSIS: Many have interpreted this case as allowing copying for use as opposed to copying for explanatory purposes. However, in applying this rule, some courts have gone a bit far and have allowed something to pass as copying for use when there were other arrangement of words available that could just as easily have been used to convey the noncopyrightable system or art. This has engendered much criticism of the aforementioned interpretation of the rule of this case.

NOTES:

RUSSELL v. PRICE

612 F.2d 1123, 205 U.S.P.Q. 206 (9th Cir. 1979).

NATURE OF CASE: Appeal of award of damages for breach of contract.

FACT SUMMARY: The holders of the copyright on the play "Pygmalion" sought to enforce the copyright against unauthorized use of a film in the public domain which was based on the play.

CONCISE RULE OF LAW: The copyright holder of a play may enforce the copyright against unauthorized exhibition of a film in the public domain which was based on the play.

FACTS: In 1913, George Bernard Shaw copyrighted the play "Pygmalion." In 1938, MGM produced a film version thereof. In 1966, the copyright expired on the film; the play's copyright was renewed in 1941 up to and including 1988. In 1975, Janus Films (P), exclusive licensee of film rights from the copyright holders of the play, discovered that Budget Films (D) was renting out copies of the film for exhibition. Janus (P) sued for infringement. The district court awarded damages, and Budget (D) appealed.

ISSUE: May the copyright holder of a play enforce the copyright against unauthorized exhibition of a film in the public domain which was based on the play?

HOLDING AND DECISION: (Goodwin, J.) Yes. The copyright holder of a play may enforce the copyright against unauthorized exhibition of a film in the public domain which was based on the play. It is well-established doctrine that a derivative copyright protects only the new material contained in the derivative work, not the matter taken from the underlying work. Thus, although derivative work may enter the public domain, the matter contained therein which derives from a work still copyrighted is subject to the copyright of the original work. Here, although the copyright to the film "Pygmalion" had expired, the material contained therein was still the property of the copyright holders to the play, and Budget (D) did not have a legal right to exhibit the film without authorization. Affirmed.

EDITOR'S ANALYSIS: A contrary result was reached by the Second Circuit in Rohauer v. Killiam Shows, Inc., 551 F.2d 484 (2d Cir. 1977), which involved a novel and film rights. The facts of this case were so different, however, that it cannot be accurately said to conflict with the instant case. That case involved an unusual confluence of survivorship and intent that limited its precedential value.

NOTES:

COLUMBIA PICTURES INDUSTRIES, INC. v. REDD HORNE, INC.

749 F.2d 154, 224 U.S.P.Q. 641 (3d Cir. 1984).

NATURE OF CASE: Appeal of order enjoining copyright infringement and awarding damages.

FACT SUMMARY: Redd Horne, Inc. (D), a video rental outlet proprietor, also exhibited videos to the public without authorization.

CONCISE RULE OF LAW: A video rental proprietor may not exhibit videos to the public without authorization.

FACTS: Redd Horne, Inc. (D) operated a videocassette rental outlet. In addition, it offered a service wherein patrons could reserve a small booth to watch videotapes in small groups. Redd Horne (D) did not obtain copyright holder authorization for this. Columbia Pictures Industries, Inc. (P) brought a copyright infringement suit. The district court issued an injunction and awarded damages and Redd Horne (D) appealed.

ISSUE: May a video rental outlet proprietor exhibit videos to the public without authorization?

HOLDING AND DECISION: (Re, C.J.) No. A video rental outlet proprietor may not exhibit videos to the public without authorization. Section 106 of the Copyright Act prohibits, in the case of motion pictures and other audiovisual works, unauthorized public exhibition. A videocassette recording of a film may not be a motion picture per se, but it certainly falls within the definition of audiovisual work. Here, the performance was no doubt public, so Redd Horne (D) has violated § 106. The first sale doctrine, contrary to Redd Horne's (D) contentions, does not affect this conclusion. All that this doctrine does is permit a vendee to resell a work. All other copyrights are reserved. Here, the right to prevent public exhibition is one such right. Affirmed.

EDITOR'S ANALYSIS: The rights of copyright holders are largely defined in § 106 of the Copyright Act, codified at 17 U.S.C. § 106. These include reproduction, preparation of derivative works, distribution of copies, exhibition, and display. Sometimes developments in technology make application of § 106 difficult, but courts usually do not find it hard to enforce the section.

NOTES:

SPRINGSTEEN v. PLAZA ROLLER DOME, INC.

602 F.Supp. 1113, 225 U.S.P.Q. 1008 (M.D.N.C. 1985).

NATURE OF CASE: Cross-motions for summary judgment in a copyright infringement action.

FACT SUMMARY: ASCAP (P) and several members thereof brought an infringement action against a small commercial establishment which provided background music for the enjoyment of its customers.

CONCISE RULE OF LAW: A small commercial establishment which provides background music for the enjoyment of its customers may not be committing a copyright infringement.

FACTS: Plaza Roller Dome, Inc. (D) operated a roller rink and an adjacent facility called the "Putt-Putt Course." [The case did not describe the nature of the amusements offered there.] The course was fitted with six speakers which provided background music, mostly from radio, for the enjoyment of customers. The sound system was unsophisticated, not much better than a home system. The course, which covered about 7,500 square feet, brought in only about $4,000 in revenues per year. The American Society of Composers, Authors and Publishers (ASCAP) (P), and several members thereof, brought an infringement suit against Plaza Roller (D), contending that the broadcasting of background music constituted a copyright violation. The parties made cross-motions for summary judgment.

ISSUE: May a small commercial establishment which provides background music for the enjoyment of its customers be committing a copyright infringement?

HOLDING AND DECISION: (Bullock, J.) No. A small commercial establishment which provides background music for the enjoyment of its customers may not be committing a copyright infringement. 17 U.S.C. § 110(5) creates a limited exemption from the scope of copyright laws for proprietors of commercial establishments who play music for the benefit of their customers. The section essentially allows the transmission of a copyrighted performance on a single receiving apparatus of a kind commonly used in private homes. The statute itself is not particularly enlightening as to how far it goes in scope. However, the legislative history states that factors to be considered in the analysis include size, physical arrangement, quality of the sound system, and the noise level in the facility. Here, the facility in question was relatively small for an amusement park. The sound system was not particularly good, and the outdoor nature of the facility dispersed the sound. The system, in short, did not figure prominently in the park. This court is of the opinion that the § 110(5) exemption applies. Summary judgment for Plaza Roller (D) ordered and motion to dismiss granted.

EDITOR'S ANALYSIS: The first major pronouncement in this area came with the case Twentieth Century Music Corp. v. Aiken, 422 U.S. 151 (1975). In this case, the Supreme Court carved out the small-system exemption from copyright laws as they apply to music broadcasting. Section 110(5) was enacted by Congress in response. It was a codification of the rule and also a limitation. Congress was concerned that it could be expanded to include facilities which, in its judgment, should pay for broadcasting music.

NOTES:

MIRAGE EDITIONS, INC. v. ALBUQUERQUE A.R.T. CO.

856 F.2d 1341, 8 U.S.P.Q. 2d 1171 (9th Cir. 1989).

NATURE OF CASE: Appeal of order enjoining copyright infringement.

FACT SUMMARY: Albuquerque A.R.T. Co. (D) engaged in the commercial activity of transferring copyrighted reprints of lithographs onto ceramic tiles, without the copyright holder's authorization.

CONCISE RULE OF LAW: A person cannot commercially transfer copyrighted artworks onto other surfaces without authorization.

NOTES:

FACTS: Mirage Editions, Inc. (P) was the exclusive publisher of the works of the renowned artist Patrick Nagel, as well as the co-owner of the copyrights thereon. Mirage (P) published a collection of his works entitled NAGEL: The Art of Patrick Nagel. It came to Mirage's (P) attention that Albuquerque A.R.T. Co. (D) was commercially engaged in the practice of transferring prints from the book onto ceramic tile. Mirage (P) sued for infringement. A district court issued an injunction, and A.R.T. (D) appealed.

ISSUE: May a person without authorization commercially transfer copyrighted artworks onto other surfaces?

HOLDING AND DECISION: (Brunetti, J.) No. A person cannot commercially transfer copyrighted artworks onto other surfaces without authorization. Under 17 U.S.C. § 106, the unauthorized derivative creation and distribution of copyrighted works is prohibited. A derivative work is broadly defined, at 17 U.S.C. § 101, "as any...form in which a work may be recast, transformed, or adapted." Here, the copyrighted prints were recast onto ceramic , so they were protected derivative works. Contrary to A.R.T.'s (D) assertions, the "first sale" doctrine does not help it. The doctrine permits a vendee of a copyrighted artwork to resell it without permission. However, the vendee is only allowed to resell it; he may not use it in the creation of a derivative work. Here, that is just what A.R.T. (D) has done, so the doctrine is unavailable to it. Affirmed.

EDITOR'S ANALYSIS: The first sale doctrine is probably the most significant limitation on copyright distribution powers. The doctrine, codified at 17 U.S.C. § 109(a), permits free alienation of a legitimately purchased artwork. Without this rule, the secondary art market would be seriously endangered.

SONY CORP. OF AMERICA v. UNIVERSAL CITY STUDIOS, INC.

464 U.S. 417 (1984).

NATURE OF CASE: Review of order reversing dismissal of copyright infringement action.

FACT SUMMARY: Universal City Studios (P) contended that Sony (D) contributed to copyright infringement by marketing videocassette recorders.

CONCISE RULE OF LAW: The marketing of videocassette recorders does not infringe on the copyrights of recorded works.

FACTS: In the 1970s Sony Corp. (D) began marketing the Betamax videocassette recorder, which allowed home recording of televised programs. Several holders of copyrights on televised programs brought an action seeking injunctive relief and damages for copyright infringement. The district court found that most copyright holders of televised programs did not object to home recording, and that home recording did not impair the value of the copyrights of those who did. The district court held Sony (D) not to be in violation of copyright laws. The Ninth Circuit reversed. The Supreme Court granted certiorari.

ISSUE: Does the marketing of videocassette recorders infringe on the copyrights of recorded works?

HOLDING AND DECISION: (Stevens, J.) No. The marketing of videocassette recorders does not infringe on the copyrights of recorded works. Such marketing could not directly infringe on copyrights. Rather, the contention is that, by marketing recording devices, Sony (D) contributes to infringement. However, if the act complained of has a substantial noninfringing dimension, the fact that it facilitates some infringement will not establish contributory infringement. Here, it was established at trial that most uses of the Betamax are for "time-shifting" rather than permanent storage, and that most copyright holders of televised works had no objection to such use. Further, even as to those holders who did object, no showing of any actual damages was made. In light of these facts, it is impossible not to conclude that the marketing of videocassette recorders offered substantial noninfringing uses thereof. Therefore, no infringement has occurred. Reversed.

EDITOR'S ANALYSIS: Unauthorized time-shifting may be considered an example of the "fair use" doctrine, which is codified at 17 U.S.C. § 107. This equitable doctrine allows a court to sanction an unauthorized use of a copyrighted work. Generally speaking, the use must be noncommercial to be within the ambit of § 107. Such was the case here.

NOTES:

HARPER & ROW PUBLISHERS, INC. v. NATION ENTERPRISES

471 U.S. 539 (1985).

NATURE OF CASE: Review of reversal of award of damages for copyright infringement.

FACT SUMMARY: Nation Enterprises (D) contended that its use of quotes from a yet-unpublished set of memoirs constituted fair use.

CONCISE RULE OF LAW: Publication of portions of a work soon to be published is not fair use thereof.

FACTS: Harper & Row Publishers, Inc. (P) obtained the rights to publish President Ford's memoirs, A Time to Heal. Time magazine contracted for the rights to preview the work immediately prior to publication. Prior to the publication of the article by Time magazine, Nation Enterprises (D), publisher of The Nation magazine, obtained a copy of the Ford manuscript. The Nation published an article that quoted the manuscript regarding the Nixon pardon. Time then declined to run the article it had planned and canceled its contract with Harper (P). Harper (P) sued Nation Enterprises (D) for copyright infringement. The district court awarded damages for infringement. The Second Circuit reversed, holding Nation Enterprises' (D) use to be a "fair use" under 17 U.S.C. § 107. The Supreme Court granted certiorari.

ISSUE: Is publication of portions of a work soon to be published a fair use thereof?

HOLDING AND DECISION: (O'Connor, J.) No. Publication of portions of a work soon to be published is not a fair use thereof. The notion behind the fair use doctrine as it was formulated in the common law was that one using a copyrighted work should not have to obtain a copyright holder's permission to use the copyrighted work in a situation where a reasonable copyright holder would in fact grant permission. Section 107 of the Copyright Act, which codified the doctrine, expressly noted in its legislative history that it was not intended to modify the common law. In terms of reasonableness, it is not reasonable to expect a copyright holder to allow another person to "scoop" it by publishing his material ahead of time. With respect to § 107's language, the section lists four factors to be considered in applying the doctrine. The two factors most salient here are purpose of the use and effect on the market. Normally, a fair use will not be one of economic competition with the copyright holder, which is precisely what prior publication of a copyrighted work is. Further, the effect on the market of such a use is illustrated by what happened here: it greatly lessens the market value of the copyrighted work. The conclusion therefore presents itself that, in almost all cases, prior publication of a work awaiting publication will not be a fair use. Such was the case here. Reversed.

EDITOR'S ANALYSIS: "Fair use" is a well-established common law doctrine. It was recognized by the Supreme Court as early as 1841. In Folsom v. Marsh, 9 F. Cas. 342 (1841), Justice Story permitted use of quotes by a reviewer as a "fair use." Use of quotes in criticism of a work has remained a major application of the doctrine.

NOTES:

COMMUNITY FOR CREATIVE NON-VIOLENCE v. REID

--U.S.--, 109 S.Ct. 2166, 10 U.S.P.Q.2d 1985 (1989).

NATURE OF CASE: Review of order adjudicating copyrights with respect to a sculpture.

FACT SUMMARY: Reid (D), who had created a sculpture on commission from CCNV (P), contended that since he had not been an employee of it under common-law agency principles, he owned the copyright thereon.

CONCISE RULE OF LAW: Under common-law agency principles, one who creates an artwork at the behest of another retains copyright thereon unless he was an employee of that other.

FACTS: The Community for Creative Non-Violence (CCNV) (P) was a nonprofit organization dedicated to advocacy for the cause of the homeless in the United States. It negotiated with Reid (D), a sculptor, for the latter to fashion a variation on the classic nativity scene, depicting homeless individuals. Agreement was finally made, and Reid (D) fashioned the sculpture out of a bronze-like material. The work was done by Reid (D) in his studio, with minimal direction from CCNV (P). After the unveiling, Reid (D) registered a copyright on the work. Subsequent to this, a disagreement arose between CCNV (P) and Reid (D) who had taken custody of the sculpture, over future exhibition thereof. CCNV (P) filed an action seeking to obtain possession of the work. The district court held CCNV (P) to have the right to exhibit the statute. The Federal Circuit of the Court of Appeals reversed, and the Supreme Court granted review.

ISSUE: Under common-law agency principles, does one who creates an artwork at the behest of another retain copyright thereon unless he had been an employee of that other?

HOLDING AND DECISION: (Marshall, J.) Yes. under common-law agency principles, one creating an artwork at the behest of another retains copyright thereon unless he had been an employee of that other. 17 U.S.C. § 201(a) provides that copyright ownership vests initially in the work's author, something Reid (D) in this instance indisputably was. Section 101 of the 1976 Copyright Act creates an exception to this in the case of works created "for hire." Section 101(2) mandates copyright vestiture in the case where the author is an independent contractor of another, in specific instances not applicable here. Section 101(1) provides that the work is one created "for hire" if the work is created by an employee within the scope of his employment, and this subsection is the only one which can divest Reid (D) of copyright therein. "Employee" is not defined in the section. This being so, the rule comes into play that words used in a statute will be presumed to possess their normal meanings. Contrary to CCNV's (P) assertions, "employee" is a narrower term than one over whom another exercises a measure of control. Rather, "employee" has a particular meaning, derived from common-law agency principles, wherein one party performs labor for another under circumstances in which that other exerts substantial control over the work environment on the laborer, as well as the manner of performance. Numerous factors figure in this equation, such as the level of skill required, tax treatment of the putative employee, the singleness of the assignment, and the source of the instrumentalities of the labor. Here, the work was highly skilled, Reid (D) was retained only for this single assignment, was not treated as an employee for tax purposes, and supplied his own tools and work area. The conclusion is mandated that, under agency principles, Reid (D) was not an employee of CCNV (P). Therefore, the § 101(1) exception to § 201(a) does not apply, and the copyright belongs to Reid (D). Affirmed.

EDITOR'S ANALYSIS: Sections 101(1) and 101(2) were the result of lengthy debate and compromise in Congress. Prior to 1955, any commissioned work belonged to the hiring party. For the next several years, changes in this rule were proposed numerous times. Not until 1965 was the substantive embodiment of current law enacted.

NOTES:

ODDO v. RIES

743 F.2d 630, 222 U.S.P.Q. 799 (9th Cir. 1984).

NATURE OF CASE: Appeal of award of damages for copyright infringement.

FACT SUMMARY: Ries (D), partner of Oddo (P), used articles written and condensed into a book manuscript by the latter in another book.

CONCISE RULE OF LAW: One who incorporates articles written by another to create a book infringes on the author's copyright.

FACTS: Oddo (P) entered into a partnership arrangement with Ries (D) wherein the latter was to contribute capital and marketing skills and the former his writing skills, in the creation of a book. Oddo (P), using articles he had previously written on the selected subject, as well as new material, fashioned a manuscript. Ries (D) became dissatisfied with Oddo's (P) progress and hired another writer to complete the manuscript, which he did. The manuscript was published. Oddo (P) sued Ries (D) for copyright infringement. The district court found infringement and awarded damages and attorney fees. Ries (D) appealed.

ISSUE: Does one who incorporates articles written by another to create a book infringe on the author's copyright?

HOLDING AND DECISION: (Goodwin, J.) Yes. One who incorporates articles written by another to create a book infringes on the author's copyright. The copyright of an article vests initially in the author of the contribution. The owner of the collective work (the publisher) has only a license to publish, absent a contract to the contrary. This being so, the author of an article has the right to enforce his copyright thereon. Here, Oddo (P) gave the Oddo-Ries partnership the rights to publish the articles; however, this license went only so far as the manuscript prepared by Oddo (P); Ries (D), in publishing another work containing the articles, violated Oddo's (P) copyright. [The court went on to reverse the award of attorney fees as not statutorily authorized.] Affirmed in part; reversed in part.

EDITOR'S ANALYSIS: In this particular case, Oddo (P) and Ries (D) had assigned the manuscript's copyright to the partnership. This being so, neither could have sued the other for infringement with respect to the manuscript. When a partnership owns a copyright, any partner thereof has full rights to exploit the copyright. Any overreaching by a partner must be remedied by access to partnership law, not copyright law.

NOTES:

STEVENS LINEN ASSOCIATES v. MASTERCRAFT CORP.

656 F.2d 11, 210 U.S.P.Q. 865 (2d Cir. 1981).

NATURE OF CASE: Appeal of issuance of injunction against and order denying damages for copyright infringement.

FACT SUMMARY: A district court declined to award a copyright infringement plaintiff compensatory damages because they involved an element of speculation.

CONCISE RULE OF LAW: That damages in a copyright infringement action involve an element of speculation does not render them unawardable.

FACTS: Stevens Linen Associates (P) began the manufacture of a type of fabric it called "Chestertown." The design was copyrighted. Subsequent to this, Mastercraft Corp. (D) introduced two designs, "Rio Grande" and "Grand Canyon." Stevens (P) sued for copyright infringement. At trial, Stevens (P) introduced evidence that its average sales dipped after Mastercraft (D) introduced its competing products, and also evidence that customers of Stevens (P) switched to Mastercraft (D). The district court found infringement, issued an injunction, and awarded attorney fees. It declined to award compensatory damages on the basis that Stevens' (P) lost sales were speculative. Stevens (P) appealed this portion of the award.

ISSUE: Does the fact that damages in a copyright infringement action involve an element of speculation render them unawardable?

HOLDING AND DECISION: (Lumbard, J.) No. That damages in a copyright infringement action involve an element of speculation does not render them unawardable. 17 U.S.C. § 504 allows an award in an infringement action of the copyright owner's actual damages, which amount to lost sales. In establishing lost sales due to infringement, a court must of necessity engage in some speculation, so the fact that such damages involve an element of speculation does not render them unawardable. Here, Stevens (P) introduced at least two substantial measures of lost sales: evidence that its average sales dipped during the period of infringement, and evidence that its customers switched to the offending products. Either method of computing damages is legitimate, and the district court, on remand, should use whichever method produces the highest figure. Reversed.

EDITOR'S ANALYSIS: As stated in the opinion, damages in an infringement action are governed by 17 U.S.C. § 504. This section allows a successful plaintiff to recover both lost profits or restitutionary damages. In the instant case, Mastercraft (D) had lost money on the competing products, so restitution was unavailable.

NOTES:

CREAM RECORDS, INC. v. JOSEPH SCHLITZ BREWING CO.

754 F.2d 826, 225 U.S.P.Q. 896 (9th Cir. 1985).

NATURE OF CASE: Appeal of award of damages for copyright infringement.

FACT SUMMARY: The Joseph Schlitz Brewing Co. (D) appropriated a small portion of a song whose copyright belonged to Cream Records, Inc. (P).

CONCISE RULE OF LAW: A copyright holder is entitled to the full value of an infringed copyright, even if only a small portion of the copyrighted work is appropriated.

FACTS: Cream Records, Inc. (P) owned the copyright to the theme song from the movie "Shaft." The Joseph Schlitz Brewing Co. (D) approached Cream (P) about a license to use the theme in a commercial. The negotiations broke down. Nonetheless, Schlitz (D) aired a commercial which featured a few bars from the song. This lead to the end of negotiations between Cream (P) and another entity wishing to use the song. Cream (P) sued for infringement. The district court found the full license value of the song to be $80,000. The court awarded $12,000 damages, or 15% of this value, because Schlitz (D) had used only a small portion of the song in its commercial. The court also awarded $5,000 restitutionary damages. Cream (P) appealed both aspects of the verdict.

ISSUE: Is a copyright holder entitled to the full value of an infringed copyright, even if only a small portion of the copyrighted work is appropriated?

HOLDING AND DECISION: (Per Curiam) Yes. A copyright holder is entitled to the full value of an infringed copyright, even if only a small portion of the copyrighted work is appropriated. Where the unauthorized use of a copyrighted work destroys the full value of that work, the owner thereof is entitled to that full value. This is true even if something less than the entire work is appropriated. Here, only a small portion of the theme from "Shaft" was wrongfully used. However, evidence showed that the identification in the public mind of the theme with Schlitz's (D) product that the unauthorized use engendered made the copyright on the work valueless. Consequently, Schlitz's (D) infringement cost Cream (P) the full value of the copyright, which was shown to be $80,000. This was the proper damage amount. [The court affirmed the award with respect to restitution.] Reversed and remanded.

EDITOR'S ANALYSIS: 17 U.S.C. § 504 was enacted in 1976. It resolved certain long-standing questions regarding damages in infringement actions. There had been much uncertainty as to whether compensatory and restitutionary damages were alternative or cumulative. Section 504 established that they would be cumulative, with the important limitation that profits used in computing damages would not be part of the amount restituted. If this were not so, double recovery would be the norm.

NOTES:

SEE v. DURANG

711 F.2d 141, 219 U.S.P.Q. 771 (9th Cir. 1983).

NATURE OF CASE: Appeal of summary judgment dismissing copyright infringement action.

FACT SUMMARY: Durang (D) wrote a play containing scenes which paralleled scenes in a play written by See (P) but which also dealt with similar ideas.

CONCISE RULE OF LAW: If a subsequent work contains scenes necessarily flowing from ideas found in a prior work, no infringement exists.

FACTS: See (P) wrote a play, "Fear of Acting," about an acting understudy. Durang (D) subsequently wrote a play based on the same subject matter, "The Actor's Nightmare." See (P) sued Durang (D) for infringement, contending that the latter work contained scenes of substantial similarity to his. The district court dismissed, ruling that the scenes in each play necessarily flowed from the concepts of the plays. See (P) appealed.

ISSUE: Does infringement exist if a subsequent work contains scenes necessarily flowing from ideas found in a prior work?

HOLDING AND DECISION: (Per Curiam) No. If a subsequent work contains scenes necessarily flowing from ideas found in a prior work, no infringement exists. Ideas cannot be copyrighted; only the expression thereof may be. Where, in the context of a dramatic work, a certain scene or event is logically compelled by the idea with which the work deals, the scene or event is considered part of the noncopyrightable idea. Here, the two plays in question both dealt with problems encountered by acting understudies. The district court concluded that the alleged similar scenes all were necessary compliments to the ideas behind the respective plays. This being the case, infringement, as a matter of law, could not have occurred. The case was therefore properly dismissed. Affirmed.

EDITOR'S ANALYSIS: The vehicle for dismissal in this instance was summary judgment. Whether or not infringement has occurred is generally a question of fact. Consequently, summary judgment is usually inappropriate. However, when the evidence is so one-sided that reasonable minds cannot differ, the vehicle may be employed.

NOTES:

NICHOLS v. UNIVERSAL PICTURES CORP.
45 F.2d 119, 7 U.S.P.Q. 84 (2d Cir. 1930).

NATURE OF CASE: Appeal from dismissal of suit for copyright infringement.

FACT SUMMARY: Universal's (D) movie, entitled "The Cohens and the Kellys," about a marriage between a Jewish and an Irish family, prompted Nichols (P) to bring suit for copyright infringement of her play "Abie's Irish Rose."

CONCISE RULE OF LAW: Copyright protection of literary property is not limited to protecting merely the literal text of the work.

FACTS: Nichols (P) authored and copyrighted the play "Abie's Irish Rose." This work depicted the marriage between a Jewish boy and an Irish Catholic girl, their deception of their religious fathers, and the eventual acceptance and reconciliation. Universal Pictures (D) produced "The Cohens and the Kellys," a movie about the marriage between an Irish boy and a Jewish girl. While not emphasizing the religious, the movie centered on the interactions of the two families. Nichols (P) brought suit for copyright infringement and the district court dismissed; Nichols (P) now appeals.

ISSUE: Is copyright protection of literary property limited merely to protecting the literal text of the work?

HOLDING AND DECISION: (Hand, J.) No. Copyright protection cannot be limited to the literal text, else a plagiarist could escape liability by immaterial variations, however, protection cannot extend to the "ideas" of the copyrighted work. Every work can be abstracted on several levels. These abstractions range from the most general statement of what the work is about to the very specific reproduction of the work. Between this series of abstractions lies the boundary between protection and non-protectable "ideas." Nobody has ever been able to fix that boundary and nobody ever can. In the case at bar, the only matter common to the two works is a quarrel between a Jewish and an Irish father, the marriage of their children, the birth of grandchildren, and a reconciliation. This is too generalized an abstraction from what Nichols (P) wrote, and thus was only a part of her "ideas." Affirmed.

EDITOR'S ANALYSIS: Copyright protects an author from infringement of his "expression" but not from appropriation of his mere "ideas." The problem is to draw the line between idea and expression, and several methods are utilized. The Nichols court utilized the "abstractions test," a test still popular among courts. Other possible approaches include the Content Analysis test (counting the number of times identical words or phrases appear — see 37 Cornell L.Q. 638 (1952)) and the "Patterns test" (comparing the sequence of events and the interplay of characters); see 45 Colum. L.Rev. 503 (1945).

NOTES:

SELLE v. GIBB

741 F.2d 896, 223 U.S.P.Q. 195 (7th Cir. 1984).

NATURE OF CASE: Action for copyright infringement.

FACT SUMMARY: The district court granted a judgment n.o.v. for the Gibb Brothers (D) on the ground that Selle (P) had not shown they had access to the song whose copyright he alleged they had infringed.

CONCISE RULE OF LAW: In order for the striking similarity between a copyrighted work and an allegedly infringing work to establish a reasonable inference of access to the copyrighted work, it must be shown that the similarity is of a type which will preclude any explanation other than that of copying.

FACTS: Selle (P) convinced a jury that the Gibb Brothers (D), better known as the Bee Gees, had infringed his copyright on a song called "Let It End." Their allegedly infringing song was the hit from the movie "Saturday Night Fever," entitled "How Deep Is Your Love." The district judge, however, granted the Gibbs' (D) motion for judgment notwithstanding the verdict and, in the alternative, for a new trial. He focused on the lack of any evidence that the Gibbs (D) had access to the copyrighted work. A classical music expert had testified to the many striking similarities in the songs, but he declined to say that the similarities could only have resulted from copying. On appeal, Selle (P) argued that access could be inferred from the striking similarity of the songs.

ISSUE: To establish a reasonable inference of access to the copyrighted work, must the striking similarity between a copyrighted work and an allegedly infringing work be of such a type as would preclude any explanation other than that of copying?

HOLDING AND DECISION: (Cudahy, C.J.) Yes. Copyright infringement can be demonstrated in the absence of any direct evidence of access, access being one means of showing that the defendant copied the copyrighted composition. Such copyright must be proved to establish copyright infringement. An inference of access can be established circumstantially by proof of similarity which is so striking that the possibilities of independent creation, coincidence, and prior common source are, as a practical matter, precluded. In this case, the availability of the copyrighted song was virtually de minimis and the expert did not state that the similarities could only be the result of copying. Affirmed.

EDITOR'S ANALYSIS: On the opposite side, a finding of significant dissimilarities will not necessarily avoid a finding of infringement. In fact, in some cases, the dissimilarities have been so suspicious as to indicate they were interjected simply to disguise deliberate copying of other portions of the composition.

NOTES:

STEINBERG v. COLUMBIA PICTURES INDUSTRIES, INC.

663 F.Supp 706, 3 U.S.P.Q.2d 1593 (S.D.N.Y. 1987).

NATURE OF CASE: Motion for summary adjudication of liability in a copyright infringement action.

FACT SUMMARY: Columbia Pictures (D) used, in a clearly recognizable fashion, an illustration by Steinberg (P) as a model for a film poster.

CONCISE RULE OF LAW: A visual image that would be recognized by the average person as having been appropriated from a copyright work infringes on that copyright.

FACTS: In 1976, Steinberg created a drawing which was used as a cover illustration by The New Yorker magazine. The drawing depicted, in humorous fashion, New York's self-perceived image as the center of the world. Specifically, it depicted a westward-looking landscape which featured portions of Manhattan Island in relative detail, and depicted in increasingly minimalist fashion, the rest of the nation, the Pacific Ocean and the Asian land mass. In 1984, Columbia Pictures (D), as an advertising campaign promoting the film "Moscow on the Hudson," distributed a poster. The poster showed in similar fashion, a relatively detailed Manhattan in the foreground. In the background, looking eastward, was a less detailed Atlantic Ocean and Europe, with a large Kremlin in the background. The Manhattan buildings in the foreground were stylistically similar to those in Steinberg's (D) drawing. Steinberg (D) sued for infringement. He moved summary adjudication as to liability.

ISSUE: Does a visual image that would be recognized by the average person as having been appropriated from a copyrighted work infringe on that copyright?

HOLDING AND DECISION: (Stanton, J.) Yes. A visual image that would be recognized by the average person as having been appropriated from a copyrighted work infringes on that copyright. To prevail in a copyright infringement action concerning a visual representation, a plaintiff must prove copying. The standard for determining whether a copying occurred is whether there is a "substantial similarity" between the works. The test for determining whether such similarity exists is whether an average lay observer would recognize the alleged copy as having been appropriated from the copyrighted work. It is not necessary that every detail be similar; as long as the appropriation is apparent, infringement exists. Here, it is more than evident that the Columbia (D) poster appropriates from the Steinberg (P) drawing. They both feature a detailed Manhattan backed by an increasingly less-detailed rest of the world in the background. Even the detailed buildings in the foreground are similar. Finally, this is not an instance of an improper attempt by Steinberg (P) to copyright the idea of New York as the center of the world. The drawing was Steinberg's expression of that idea, which was a proper subject of copyright. Motion granted.

EDITOR'S ANALYSIS: The Second Circuit, the circuit in which the district court here sat, once had a different test. This was called the "ordinary observer" test. As articulated by Learned Hand, the test would be met if, to an ordinary observer, the pictures had the same aesthetic appeal. The test as it is now stated would appear to be somewhat more favorable to plaintiffs.

NOTES:

GROSS v. SELIGMAN

212 F. 930 (2d Cir. 1914).

NATURE OF CASE: Appeal from injunction for infringement of copyright.

FACT SUMMARY: Seligman (D) published a photograph of a nude young woman in a pose very similar to that of an earlier picture, photographed and copyrighted by the same artist, that copyright being owned by Gross (P).

CONCISE RULE OF LAW: Where the original artist uses a work whose rights he has granted to another to produce a subsequent but marginally different work, the subsequent work is a copy and the artist an infringer.

FACTS: Rochlitz, an artist, posed a model in the nude and produced a photograph which he named "Race Of Youth." A copyright was obtained and sold to Gross (P). Two years later, Rochlitz placed the same model in the identical pose with the single exception that the young woman wore a smile and held a cherry stem between her teeth. This photograph, "Cherry Ripe," published by Seligman (D), was enjoined as an infringement of Gross' (P) copyright. Seligman (D) appeals.

ISSUE: If an artist who has granted all rights in a work to another then uses that work to produce a subsequent but marginally different work, is the subsequent work a copy and the artist an infringer?

HOLDING AND DECISION: (Lacombe, J.) Yes. If an author grants all his rights to another person but then attempts to reproduce the identical work with but slight differences, it is a copy and he is an infringer. This is not the case if the subsequent work, although substantially similar, was independently created without reference to the prior work. However, where the first work was used to produce the second, that work is a copy. Here, there were differences between the two photographs but the identities were much greater than the differences. It appeared that Rochlitz was careful to introduce only enough differences to argue about, while undertaking to make what would seem to be a copy to the ordinary purchaser who did not have both photographs before him at the same time. Offering such photograph for sale infringed Gross' (P) copyright. Affirmed.

EDITOR'S ANALYSIS: The test of infringement is twofold. Copying exists where the infringer has had access to the original work of art and where the subsequent work is substantially similar to the first. The access does not have to be actual, deliberate, or in bad faith and it may be inferred by the courts. The substantial similarity branch of the test is subject to broad judicial discretion because it must be proven that the author actually copies the prior work, by not acting independently and imaginatively, and that such copying was not permissible. Without access, the question of substantial similarity is not considered.

NOTES:

GILLIAM v. AMERICAN BROADCASTING COMPANIES, INC.

538 F.2d 14, 192 U.S.P.Q. 1 (2d Cir. 1976).

NATURE OF CASE: Appeal of denial of injunction in copyright infringement action.

FACT SUMMARY: A comedy troupe contended that broadcasting edited versions of their comedy routines constituted copyright infringement.

CONCISE RULE OF LAW: Unauthorized editing of a televised program for broadcasting constitutes copyright infringement.

FACTS: In the early 1970s a controversial comedy troupe, Monty Python's Flying Circus, appeared in a self-titled series on the BBC, which consisted of numerous skits, sketches, and blackouts. Subsequent to this, American Broadcasting Companies (ABC) (D) obtained the rights to air several episodes. ABC (D) planned to air two ninety-minute compilations of Python episodes. Unbeknownst to the troupe members, ABC (D) made substantial changes, editing out over 25% of the material for both commercial and editorial reasons. After the first telecast, Gilliam (P) and the other Python members sought an injunction against further broadcast, contending that the excisions constituted copyright infringement. The district court denied the injunction, and Gilliam (P) appealed.

ISSUE: Does unauthorized editing of a television program for broadcasting constitute copyright infringement?

HOLDING AND DECISION: (Lumbard, J.) Yes. Unauthorized editing of a television program for broadcasting constitutes copyright infringement. A recorded television program may be regarded as a work derived from its underlying script. The copyright holder of the script retains control over all uses of the script, even the recorded program itself. Consequently, to the extent that the scriptwriter has not parted with his copyright control, he had the copyright to the recorded version thereof. One who obtains permission to use a copyrighted script may not exceed the limits granted by the copyright holder. Where a licensee is granted permission to air a derivative work, this license does not automatically confer the right to edit the work. The ability of a copyright holder to control use of his work is paramount in copyright law, and the right to edit must be expressly granted. Here, ABC (D) was given permission to air certain Python material, but was not given permission to edit the material. Its doing so violated the copyright on the work. Further, such unauthorized editing constitutes mutilation of an original work, in violation of § 43(a) of the Lanham Act. [The court analyzed the traditional requisites for a preliminary injunction. It found that ABC's (D) actions had irreparably harmed Python's reputation, and that Gilliam (P) would likely succeed on the merits. It therefore ordered the district court to issue on injunction against further edited rebroadcasting.]

CONCURRENCE: (Gurfein, J.) The Lanham Act deals with trademarks not copyrights, and should not have been invoked here.

EDITOR'S ANALYSIS: As stated in the concurrence, § 43(a) of the Lanham Act was enacted to deal with trademarks, as was the entire Lanham Act. The Act is essentially a federal counterpart to state unfair competition laws, which prohibit the representation of a product as something it is not. It was applied here on the theory that ABC (D) was offering a "product" (the telecast) as a Python work, something it no longer was because of the editing.

NOTES:

WHELAN ASSOCIATES, INC. v. JASLOW DENTAL LABORATORY, INC.

797 F.2d 1222 (3d Cir. 1986).

NATURE OF CASE: Appeal of award of damages for copyright infringement.

FACT SUMMARY: Whelan Associates (P) contended that Jaslow Dental Laboratories (D) copied the structure of a computer program on which it possessed a copyright.

CONCISE RULE OF LAW: The structure of a computer program is copyrightable.

FACTS: Jaslow Dental Laboratories (D) contracted with Strohl Systems for the latter to design a program for organizing a dental lab. The agreement provided that Strohl was to own the copyright on any program created. Whelan (P), a Strohl employee, investigated the workings of Jaslow's (D) lab and created a program she named Dentalab. Strohl licensed Jaslow (D) to use the program and marketed it in the dental lab industry. Whelan (P) eventually purchased the copyright and formed Whelan Associates, Inc. (P) to further market the program. Jaslow (D) subsequently wrote a program similar to Dentalab in a different computer language, BASIC, which was more widely used in small computers than Dentalab's language, EDL. Whelan (P) sued for copyright infringement. The district court found infringement and awarded damages. Jaslow (D) appealed, contending that the structure of a program could not be copyrighted, only the program's literal code.

ISSUE: Is the structure of a computer program copyrightable?

HOLDING AND DECISION: (Becker, J.) Yes. The structure of a computer program is copyrightable. A computer program consists both of a structure and a literal code. The structure is the manner in which the steps the computer will take are arranged. The literal code is the actual sequencing of binary numbers into the computer, which constitutes the programming of the computer. It is not contended here that Jaslow (D) copied the code; however, Whelan (P) contended, and the district court found, that Jaslow (D) copied the structure. Jaslow (D) contends that structure cannot be copyrighted. While the issue involves novel technology, recourse must be made to traditional copyright law principles. Ideas may be copyrighted; expressions thereof may not. Consequently, the issue turns on whether structure is an idea or an expression. With respect to utilitarian works, the purpose or function of the work is the idea, and everything not necessary to that function is expression. With respect to computer programs, the idea would be the purpose underlying a program; everything done to attain that purpose would be expression. It would appear that numerous structures could be utilized to attain that purpose. Therefore, the structure of a program is an expression which may be copyrighted, as the district so held. [The court went on to hold that the district court's conclusion that Jaslow's (D) program was substantially similar to Dentalab and that infringement had occurred was supported by substantial evidence.]

EDITOR'S ANALYSIS: "Substantial similarity" is the universal test of whether an infringement occurs in copyright. Usually, substantial similarity has both an "extrinsic" (expert opinion) component and an "intrinsic" (lay juror opinion) component. In the case of highly technical copyrights, many courts dispense with the intrinsic component. The court did so here.

NOTES:

PLAINS COTTON COOP. ASSOC. v. GOODPASTURE COMP.

807 F.2d 1256 (5th Cir. 1987); cert. denied 484 U.S. 821 (1987).

NATURE OF CASE: Appeal from denial of injunctive relief.

FACT SUMMARY: Injunctive relief was denied Plains (P) based upon its failure to show a substantial likelihood of success in an ultimate copyright infringement suit against Goodpasture (D).

CONCISE RULE OF LAW: Injunctive relief from copyright infringement requires a showing of copyrightability and substantial similarity between two properties.

FACTS: Plains (P), a cotton grower's cooperative, developed a computer program based on data used in the cotton industry. Goodpasture (D), who worked on the program while employed by Plains (P), formed his own company, which began marketing a substantially similar program. Plains (P) sought an injunction against the further marketing of the program on the basis that it infringed on its copyright. The trial court denied the petition, finding Plains (P) had not met its burden of establishing a substantial likelihood of success at trial and the ability of the work to be protected by copyright.

ISSUE: Does injunctive relief from copyright infringement require a showing of a substantial likelihood of success at trial and of the ability of the property to be protected by copyright?

HOLDING AND DECISION: (Williams, J.) Yes. Injunctive relief from copyright infringement requires a showing of a substantial likelihood of success at trial and that the property is of a nature that can be protected by copyright. The findings of the trial court on these issues are discretionary and must be upheld unless clearly erroneous. The district court weighed the evidence of substantial similarity between the two systems both in terms of direct copying and organizational copying. Based upon testimonial and expert evidence, the court determined that no substantial likelihood was established that Plains (P) would prevail at trial on the main issue of substantial similarity. Further, although there is authority to the contrary, the trial court held the program may not be protected by copyright. As a result, no abuse of discretion was shown. Affirmed.

EDITOR'S ANALYSIS: The procedural posture of this case played a large role in the court's refusal to adopt or reject a blanket rule concerning the ability of computer programs to be copyrighted. The petition for injunctive relief calls upon the court merely to determine the likelihood of success at trial of the petitioner. The court did not want to establish such a wide-ranging rule which would go beyond its necessary role in the case.

NOTES:

BRODERBUND SOFTWARE, INC. v. UNISON WORLD, INC.

648 F.Supp 1127, 231 U.S.P.Q. 700 (N.D.Cal 1986).

NATURE OF CASE: Action for damages and injunctive relief for copyright infringement.

FACT SUMMARY: Unison World (D) contended that, in the context of computer software, menu screens, input formats, and sequencing of screens are noncopyrightable ideas.

CONCISE RULE OF LAW: In the context of computer software, menu screens, input formats, and sequencing of screens are copyrightable.

FACTS: Broderbund Software (P) was an exclusive licensee of a software program developed by Pixellite Software (P) called "The Print Shop." This particular program allowed computers to generate greeting cards. The program was compatible only with Apple computers. At one point, Unison World, Inc. (D) began negotiating for the right to develop an IBM-compatible version of "Print Shop." Its technicians were instructed to copy as much as possible the features of "Print Shop." Negotiations were never consummated, but Unison (D) brought out its program nonetheless, calling it "Printmaster." "Printmaster" featured basically the same function as "Print Shop," employing essentially the same menu screens, input formats, and sequencing of screens. Broderbund (P) and Pixellite (P) sued for infringement. At trial, evidence was introduced of a program called "Stickybear Printer," which permitted the printing of greeting cards in a manner dissimilar to "Print Shop." Expert testimony regarding similarity was also introduced. Unison (D) argued that menu screens, input formats, and screen sequencing were noncopyrightable ideas.

ISSUE: In the context of computer software, are menu screens, input formats, and sequencing of screens copyrightable ideas?

HOLDING AND DECISION: (Orrick, J.) Yes. In the context of computer software, menu screens, input formats, and sequencing of screens are copyrightable ideas. It is axiomatic that ideas may not be copyrighted, but expression thereof may be, unless the expression is a necessary corollary to the noncopyrightable idea. Therefore, menu screens, input formats, and sequencing of screens are copyrightable if they are not dictated by the idea underlying the program. Here, the underlying idea is that of computer-generated greeting cards. Unison (D) argued that the way "Print Shop" worked, its menu screens, input formats, and sequencing of screens was the only logical way to do so, and therefore it could not have violated copyright thereon. However, "Stickybear Printer" was introduced into evidence, demonstrating that a program could fulfill the same function as "Print Shop," but in a dissimilar manner. Therefore, Unison's (D) contentions in this regard were contrary to the factual record. Menu screens, input formats, and sequencing of screens were copyrightable here. [The court went on to hold substantial similarity to have been present and for infringement to have therefore occurred.]

EDITOR'S ANALYSIS: Unison's (D) argument largely admitted substantial similarity, so the court did not dwell on its analysis thereof. The test for substantial similarity in expression is what is called the "intrinsic test." That test asks whether the alleged infringing work captures the total concept and feel of the senior work. If the answer is in the affirmative, the junior work infringes the copyright of the senior work.

NOTES:

VAULT CORPORATION v. QUAID SOFTWARE LIMITED

847 F.2d 255, 7 U.S.P.Q.2d 1281 (5th Cir. 1988).

NATURE OF CASE: Appeal of denial of damages and injunctive relief for copyright infringement.

FACT SUMMARY: Quaid Software (D) marketed a computer diskette which neutralized an anti-copying device incorporated onto diskettes manufactured by Vault Corporation (P).

CONCISE RULE OF LAW: A diskette which neutralizes an anti-copying device incorporated onto another diskette does not violate the copyright on that diskette.

FACTS: Vault Corporation (P) manufactured floppy diskettes used by computer software concerns on which to imprint their programs. A key feature of the diskettes was called "PROLOK." This feature supposedly prevented copying of the programs encoded on the diskettes. In response, Quaid Software Limited (D) designed and marketed a diskette with a feature called "RAMKEY" which neutralized the PROLOK function of Vault's (P) diskettes. In order to make RAMKEY diskettes, it was necessary to reproduce PROLOK's program during the manufacturing process. Vault (P) sued for infringement. A district court denied a preliminary injunction, and the order was made final. Vault (P) appealed.

ISSUE: Does a diskette which neutralizes an anti-copying device incorporated onto another diskette violate the copyright on that diskette?

HOLDING AND DECISION: (Reavley, J.) No. A diskette which neutralizes an anti-copying device incorporated onto another diskette does not violate the copyright on that diskette. Since the latter device must of necessity involve the copying of the program of the former device, the issue arises as to whether such copying constitutes infringement. Section 117 of the 1976 Copyright Act (as amended in 1980) provides that the possessor of a copyrighted computer program may lawfully copy it if (1) such use is an essential step in utilizing the program, or (2) such copy is for archival purposes only. In the instance of copying a program for the purpose of creating a program that cancels it, it appears that such a practice falls within the ambit of § 117(1). Vault (P) urges an interpretation of the subsection permitting copying only for the copyright holder's intended use. However, it is not the function of a court to create statutory language where it is not found. Since the copying here was essential for its use, no infringement occurred. Alternatively, Vault (P) argues that Quaid (D), in its marketing of RAMKEY, contributes to infringement of copyrighted matters placed on diskettes by Vault's (P) processes. However, it is clearly demonstrable that RAMKEY may be used to defeat PROLOK for legitimate archiving purposes, as permitted by § 117(2). Since a substantial noninfringing use exists, no copyright violation has occurred. Affirmed.

EDITOR'S ANALYSIS: Contributory infringement was discussed by the Supreme Court in Sony Corp. of America v. Universal City Studios, 464 U.S. 417 (1984). There, it was contended that Sony, by marketing VCRs and videotapes, encouraged copyright violations. The Supreme Court struck down a Ninth Circuit decision so holding, finding that the presence of a substantial noninfringing use, "time shifting," militated against a finding of contributing infringement.

NOTES:

DIAMOND v. DIEHR

450 U.S. 175 (1981).

NATURE OF CASE: Review of order reversing Patent Office rejection of patent application.

FACT SUMMARY: Diehr (P) sought to patent a process for curing synthetic rubber which included in several of its steps the use of a mathematical formula and a programmed digital computer.

CONCISE RULE OF LAW: A process which includes in several of its steps the use of a mathematical formula and a programmed digital computer may be patentable.

FACTS: The rubber industry had long encountered a problem in the heat curing of synthetic rubber in that, although an equation existed for determining how long the curing should last, the temperature of the mold had been an unquantifiable variable. Diehr (P) developed a process in which the molds used for curing constantly relayed temperature information to a digital computer, which employed the equation to determine when the curing process should end. Diehr (P) applied for a patent. The Patent Office denied the application on the basis that it involved matters not patentable under 35 U.S.C. § 101. The Patent and Trademark Board of Appeals affirmed, but the Court of Customs and Patent Appeals reversed. The Government (D) petitioned for certiorari.

ISSUE: May a process which includes in several of its steps the use of a mathematical formula and a programmed digital computer be patentable?

HOLDING AND DECISION: (Rehnquist, J.) Yes. A process which includes in several of its steps the use of a mathematical formula and a programmed digital computer may be patentable. 35 U.S.C. § 101 allows to be patented any "new and useful process." A process is a mode of treatment of certain materials to produce a given result. This is a broad definition, and the subject matter at issue here certainly falls within this definition. It is true that the process at issue here employs a mathematical formula, and a digital computer which utilizes the formula. A mathematical formula cannot be patented, as it is a manifestation of nature. Things which are such manifestations of nature, separate from human endeavors, cannot be patented. However, it does not flow from this that a process which employs a mathematical formula is unpatentable. While the formula cannot be patented, the rest of the process may be. Here, the rubber curing process at issue contained components other than the formula, and for this reason was within the patentability scope of § 101. Affirmed.

DISSENT: (Stevens, J.) The Court's focus is entirely wrong. Diehr (P) has invented nothing new regarding the chemistry of synthetic rubber curing, nothing new regarding the materials used therefor, and nothing about the significance or effect of any process variable. What he has done is applied a mathematical formula to a series of steps which are well within the state of the rubber curing art and employed a computer utilizing the formula. Precedents of this Court imply, and the Court should explicitly now hold, that no program-related invention is a patentable process under § 101 unless it makes a contribution to the art that is not dependent solely upon the utilization of a computer.

EDITOR'S ANALYSIS: The rule that "manifestations of nature" could not be patented is quite old, and for a long period of time did not present much of a problem in application. It was used as a basis for denying patent applications for minerals and vegetation. As the present case demonstrates, the computer revolution has made application of the doctrine more difficult.

NOTES:

JOSTENS, INC. v. NATIONAL COMPUTER SYSTEMS, INC.

Minn. Sup. Ct., 318 N.W.2d 691, 214 U.S.P.Q. 918 (1982).

NATURE OF CASE: Appeal of denial of claim of trade secret infringement and commercial misappropriation.

FACT SUMMARY: Jostens (P) contended that NCS (D) had infringed trade secrets in a computer system it had developed, but which it had not taken significant steps to keep secret.

CONCISE RULE OF LAW: Trade secret infringement may not be claimed as to a system which the claimant has not attempted to keep secret.

FACTS: Jostens (P) was a leading maker of school products, including class rings. It developed a system of producing class rings with the use of a computer system, called CAD/CAM. The system was largely developed by Titus (D), an employee. At one point Jostens (P) considered marketing the system, which was shown to several possible investors. Jostens (P) eventually decided against this course. During this period Titus (D) published, with Jostens' (P) approval, an article explaining the system. Also, Jostens (P) employees were never told that the system was a secret. Eventually, several Jostens (P) employees, including Titus (D), went to work for National Computer Systems (NCS) (D). There, a similar system was developed and eventually marketed. Jostens (P) sued NCS (D) and Titus (D) for trade secret infringement and commercial misappropriation. The trial court entered a defense verdict, and Jostens (P) appealed.

ISSUE: May trade secret infringement be claimed as to a system which the claimant has not attempted to keep secret?

HOLDING AND DECISION: (Simunett, J.) No. Trade secret infringement may not be claimed as to a system which the claimant has not attempted to keep secret. One of the essential elements of a trade secret course of action is a demonstrable intent by the developer/owner to keep the process secret. While total secrecy may not be required in all cases, the owner must have evidenced a desire not to make the information public. In this instance, the trial court found, and the evidence supports that Jostens (P) did not do this. It never instructed its employees that the system was secret; it, for a period of time, attempted to market the system, disclosing how it worked to potential buyers; finally, it allowed an employee to publish an explanatory article about the system. Together, these facts demonstrate a lack of intent to keep the system a secret. Consequently, trade secret infringement could not have occurred. The same is true with commercial misappropriation. Affirmed.

EDITOR'S ANALYSIS: The elements of trade secret infringement vary in the details from state to state, but the basic requirements are fairly consistent. They generally require that the matter not be generally known, provide a competitive advantage, be gained at the claimant's expense and be intended to be kept a secret. Some states incorporate these requirements into decisional law. Others, like Minnesota here, have enacted statutes.

NOTES:

IN RE NALBANDIAN

C.C.P.A., 661 F.2d 1214, 211 U.S.P.Q. 782 (1981).

NATURE OF CASE: Appeal of order rejecting patent application.

FACT SUMMARY: Johnson contended that the design of Nalbandian for a pair of illuminated tweezers was an improvement over his patented design which would be obvious only to a designer of such implements, not an ordinary consumer.

CONCISE RULE OF LAW: For purposes of "obviousness" as an element of a patent, the design must not have been obvious to a skilled designer of the type of product at issue.

FACTS: Nalbandian submitted a patent application for a type of illuminated tweezers he had designed. The Patent Office denied the application on the basis that the design was an obvious improvement over a patented design belonging to one Johnson. Nalbandian appealed to the Patent and Trademark Office Board of Appeals, contending that the improvement would not be obvious to the ordinary observer. The Board of Appeals affirmed, and Nalbandian appealed. Johnson contended that the improvement was obvious to one skilled in the design of such implements.

ISSUE: For purposes of "obviousness" as an element of a patent, must the design not have been obvious to a skilled designer of the type of product at issue?

HOLDING AND DECISION: (Nies, J.) Yes. For purposes of "obviousness" as an element of a patent, the design must not have been obvious to a skilled designer of the type of product at issue. Per 35 U.S.C. § 103, a patent will not issue as to a design which would have been obvious, at the time the invention was made, to a person having ordinary skill in the art to which the subject matter pertains. Some courts have interpreted this to mean obvious to an ordinary intelligent individual. This court disagrees, believing that it refers to an ordinary designer of the product in question. First, such an interpretation is more consistent with the statutory language. Further, the obviousness of a design with respect to a designer is more readily quantifiable than with respect to an ordinary intelligent person. Finally, this court believes that such an interpretation better effects the congressional purpose or promoting invention. Here, the design would have been obvious to a skilled designer, and therefore Nalbandian's application was properly rejected. Affirmed.

CONCURRENCE: (Rich, J.) It is time for Congress to legislatively clear up the difficulty courts have been having with the concept of obviousness, by enacting better-phrased legislation. Proposals therefor have been pending in Congress for a long time.

DISSENT: (Rich, J.) The test adopted by the court is correct, but the result is wrong. Here, Nalbandian's design was not obvious.

EDITOR'S ANALYSIS: Nonobviousness was enacted as an element to a patent in the 1952 Patent Act. The problem of ascertaining nonobviousness, however, predates that. Prior to 1952, an element of a design patent was "invention." "Nonobviousness" was substituted in 1952 for "invention." The difference between the two has proved difficult to divine.

NOTES:

AVIA GROUP INTERNATIONAL, INC. v. L.A. GEAR CALIFORNIA, INC.

853 F.2d 1557, 7 U.S.P.Q.2d 1548 (Fed. Cir. 1988).

NATURE OF CASE: Appeal of order granting summary adjudication of liability in patent infringement action.

FACT SUMMARY: L.A. Gear (D) contended that a shoe component could not be given a design patent because it was functional, not ornamental.

CONCISE RULE OF LAW: An item may be given a design patent even if it has a functional aspect.

FACTS: Avia Group International, Inc. (P) obtained two design patents on distinctively-designed shoe components. It subsequently sued L.A. Gear California (D) for patent infringement, contending that the designs had been copied. A district court found the designs substantially the same and granted summary adjudication on liability. L.A. Gear (D) appealed, contending that the patents were invalid because the components were primarily functional, not ornamental.

ISSUE: May an item be given a design patent even if it has a functional aspect?

HOLDING AND DECISION: (Nies, J.) Yes. An item may be given a design patent even if it has a functional aspect. 35 U.S.C. § 171 allows a patent to be obtained on a design which is "new, original and ornamental." L.A. Gear (D) contends that a design patent may not be given on an article which is functional rather than ornamental. This is a misreading of the section. A design patent may be issued as to the ornamental aspects of a functional article. Thus, an article will not be rendered incapable of meriting a design patent by virtue of a utilitarian application. Here, the components at issue were no doubt functional in nature. However, the design patent had been issued as to distinctive, ornamental aspects of the components, not their functions. Consequently the patents were valid. The court's finding that L.A. Gear's (D) product infringed the patent was not erroneous, and its holding was therefore correct. Affirmed.

EDITOR'S ANALYSIS: Design patents incorporate the elements of utility patents enumerated in 35 U.S.C. §§ 101-03. The extra requirement is "ornamentality." This term is not statutorily defined. Courts usually construe it as the absence of functionality. As the present case illustrates, however, an item can be both functional and ornamental.

NOTES:

MAZER v. STEIN

347 U.S. 201 (1954).

NATURE OF CASE: Review of order enjoining copyright infringement and awarding damages.

FACT SUMMARY: Mazer (D) contended that an article having a utilitarian application could not be copyrighted.

CONCISE RULE OF LAW: An article having a utilitarian application may be copyrighted.

FACTS: Stein (P) obtained a copyright on a statuette. The statuette was put into mass production and was used as a base for table lamps. Mazer (D) began producing duplicate statuettes for use in table lamps. Stein (P) brought an action alleging copyright infringement, seeking damages and injunctive relief. The district court found infringement and awarded damages and enjoined further infringement. Mazer (D) appealed, contending that a practically useful article could be protected only by a patent, not by a copyright. The court of appeals affirmed, and the Supreme Court granted certiorari.

ISSUE: Can an article having a utilitarian application be copyrighted?

HOLDING AND DECISION: (Reed, J.) Yes. An article having a utilitarian application may be copyrighted. Resolution of this issue is strictly a matter of statutory construction. Neither the patent law nor the copyright law contain any provisions excluding an item from falling within the ambit of both areas. Further, this Court sees nothing in so doing which would frustrate the purpose behind these laws which is to encourage invention and innovation. Consequently, if an article is copyrightable, the fact that it may be patentable is of no consequence. The Copyright Act explicitly includes "statues, statuary, and . . . models." Consequently, it is clear that the statuettes in question are copyrightable. This being so, their industrial application did not make Mazer's (D) copying any less an infringing act. Affirmed.

CONCURRENCE: (Douglas, J.) The Constitution only gives Congress the power to grant copyrights on "writings." Therefore, the copyright law may exceed Congress' constitutional authority. The case should be submitted for reargument and rebriefing on this issue.

EDITOR'S ANALYSIS: The Court did not address the issue of whether the statuette was patentable, as its conclusion that the statuette was copyrightable made the issue moot. Generally speaking, patentability is more difficult to achieve than copyrightability. It is questionable whether the patentability requirements of novelty, utility, and originality would have existed here.

NOTES:

CAROL BARNHART INC. v. ECONOMY COVER CORP.

773 F.2d 411, 228 U.S.P.Q. 385 (2d Cir. 1985).

NATURE OF CASE: Appeal of summary judgment dismissing copyright infringement action.

FACT SUMMARY: Carol Barnhart, Inc. (P) sought copyright protection of certain mannequins whose ornamental features were inseparable from their functional features.

CONCISE RULE OF LAW: An article whose ornamental features are inseparable from its functional features is not copyrightable.

FACTS: Carol Barnhart, Inc. (P) began marketing certain distinctive mannequins for sale to clothing retailers. Economy Cover Corp. (D) began selling duplicates. Upon learning of this, Barnhart (P) applied for and received a copyright on the mannequin design. It then sued for infringement. The district court held that the mannequins' ornamental qualities were inseparable from their function and were therefore uncopyrightable. The court therefore granted summary judgment dismissing the case. Barnhart (P) appealed.

ISSUE: Is an article whose ornamental features are inseparable from its functional features copyrightable?

HOLDING AND DECISION: (Mansfield, J.) No. An article whose ornamental features are inseparable from its functional features is not copyrightable. Under §§ 101 and 102 of the Copyright Act, pictoral, graphic and sculptural works may be copyrighted. However, they may be copyrighted only to the extent that the matter for which copyright is sought is capable of existing independently of the article's utilitarian aspects. A review of legislative, judicial, and administrative history since at least 1870 shows an increasing tendency to cover articles having a utilitarian dimension. However, all authorities have stopped short of applying copyright protection for works of applied art or industrial design which have aesthetic features that cannot be identified separately from the useful article. Here, the aesthetic features of the mannequins at issue were all derived from the manner in which they served their modeling function. Consequently, features do not have a separate existence, and cannot be copyrighted. Affirmed.

DISSENT: (Newman, J.) The separateness between function and aesthetics necessary for copyrightability is not physical, but conceptual. If, to the ordinary reasonable observer, function and aesthetics would be conceptually distinct, the ornamental features are copyrightable. Here, such an observer could admire the ornamental features without contemplating the function of the mannequins so these features should be copyrightable.

EDITOR'S ANALYSIS: It is rather difficult to reconcile the instant case with Mazer v. Stein, 347 U.S. 201 (1954). In that case, certain decorative statuettes were held to be copyrightable. It is difficult indeed to see the difference between the statuettes in Mazer and the mannequins here. It is possible that the focus of each case was different: in Mazer, the Court was occupied more with the issue of whether patentability precluded copyrightability than the issue of copyrightability itself.

NOTES:

IN RE MORTON-NORWICH PRODUCTS, INC.

U.S.C.C.P.A., 671 F.2d 1332, 213 U.S.P.Q. 9 (1982).

NATURE OF CASE: Appeal of refusal to register trademark.

FACT SUMMARY: Morton-Norwich Products (P) sought to register as a trademark the shape of a spray bottle.

CONCISE RULE OF LAW: The shape of an item may be registered as a trademark.

FACTS: Morton-Norwich Products, Inc. (P) marketed several household liquid products in a plastic spray bottle of a certain shape. The products were differentiated by labels and bottle color. Morton (P) applied for a trademark as to the bottle's shape, which included certain curves not found on competitors' products. The Patent and Trademark Office denied the application, holding that all features of the bottle advanced its utilitarian function. The Board of Appeals affirmed, and Morton (P) appealed.

ISSUE: May the shape of an item be registered as a trademark?

HOLDING AND DECISION: (Rich, J.) Yes. The shape of an item may be registered as a trademark. The only aspects of an item that cannot be registered as trademarks are those which cannot be separated from its function. However, any aspect that can be considered an unnecessary elaboration or ornamentation may be. Consequently, to the extent that the shape of a product is not completely dictated by function, that shape is copyrightable. Here, the bottle in question has a distinctive shape, containing certain curves that are not necessary to its function. Consequently, the shape of the bottle may be copyrighted, provided that the patent examiner, on remand, finds the shape to be distinctive. Reversed.

EDITOR'S ANALYSIS: In theory, functionality is not hard to define. A feature may be considered functional if it is essential to the use or purpose of the article. Despite this rather pedestrian definition, the functionality/nonfunctionality issue has often proven difficult to resolve. What is useful may often be aesthetically pleasing and, hence, the confusion.

NOTES:

KEENE CORP. v. PARAFLEX INDUSTRIES, INC.

653 F.2d 822, 211 U.S.P.Q. 201 (3d Cir. 1981).

NATURE OF CASE: Appeal of order denying injunction against alleged trademark infringement.

FACT SUMMARY: A court refused to find trademark infringement in the shape of a luminaire because the shape thereof was relevant to its purpose.

CONCISE RULE OF LAW: A distinctive feature of an article will not be trademarkable if the feature is important to its purpose.

FACTS: Keene Corp. (P) produced a type of luminaire for illuminating the outside areas adjacent to the walls of commercial buildings. The luminaires had a distinctive shape. The shape of these illuminating devices was relevant to their use, as the shapes had to be compatible with the walls upon which they were mounted. Keene (P) brought an action against Paraflex Industries (D), which had begun importing Taiwanese copies, alleging unfair competition and trademark infringement. The court found the shape of Keene's (P) products to be important to its purpose and held no trademark violation, although it did order Paraflex (D) to identify the products as being other than those made by Keene (P). Keene (P) appealed.

ISSUE: Will a distinctive feature of an article be trademarkable if the feature is important to its purpose?

HOLDING AND DECISION: (Sloviter, J.) No. A distinctive feature of an article will not be trademarkable if the feature is important to its purpose. A functional feature of an article cannot be given a trademark if it serves the functional aspect of that product even if that feature is at the same time ornamental or distinctive in some manner. A feature which is arbitrary may be given trademark protection, but if the feature is utilitarian, the fact that such utility was achieved in an aesthetically pleasing or distinctive fashion will not render it capable of trademark protection. This is what is commonly termed "aesthetic functionality." Here, there is no doubt but that the shape of Keene's (P) luminaires was distinctive. However, shape was dictated to a large extent by the functional consideration of attachability to building walls. Therefore, the shape was not arbitrary and, therefore, not capable of being given a trademark. Affirmed.

EDITOR'S ANALYSIS: All intellectual property law is to some extent anticompetitive, which is contrary to the usual thrust of the law. Aesthetic functionality represents an accommodation with the law's usual pro-competitive bias. Where the giving of a trademark will tend to stifle competition excessively, even the presence of distinctiveness will not make the article capable of being given a trademark.

NOTES:

BONITO BOATS, INC. v. THUNDER CRAFT BOATS, INC.

___ U.S. ___, 109 S. Ct 971 (1989).

NATURE OF CASE: Review of order voiding state law prohibiting duplication of boat hulls.

NOTES:

FACT SUMMARY: Thunder Craft Boats (D) contended that Florida's law prohibiting the duplication of unpatented boat hulls violated federal patent laws.

CONCISE RULE OF LAW: A state may not prohibit the duplication of unpatented or unpatentable articles.

FACTS: Florida enacted a law prohibiting the duplication of molded boat hulls. Bonito Boats, Inc. (P) which had designed a certain type of boat hull mold and had commercially exploited it, brought an action against Thunder Craft Boats, Inc. (D). Bonito (P) alleged that Thunder Craft (D) had copied the design of its hull. The design was not patented. The trial court held the Florida law to be preempted by federal patent law and declared the law invalid. The appellate and Florida Supreme Courts affirmed, and the Supreme Court granted certiorari.

ISSUE: May a state prohibit the duplication of unpatented or unpatentable articles?

HOLDING AND DECISION: (O'Connor, J.) No. A state may not prohibit the duplication of unpatented or unpatentable articles. Federal patent law reflects a very careful balance between healthy competition and rewarding innovation. A person who meets the requirements of novelty, usefulness, and nonobviousness will be rewarded with a temporary monopoly; all other utilitarian articles may be exploited by the public. Federal patent-law laws, in order to determine what is protected, must also determine what is not protected. The balance struck in patent laws requires that all nonpatented, publicly known designs be freely traded. If states were free to grant de facto monopolies to unpatented or unpatentable articles, the balance struck in federal patent laws would be upset. Here, the Florida law is a good illustration. Bonito (P) did not apply for a patent. Consequently, federal patent law would permit any competitor to use its design. The Florida law prevents this. Consequently, the Florida law acts to upset the fine balance created in patent law. Since the law is inconsistent with federal law, it must fail. Affirmed.

EDITOR'S ANALYSIS: This case should not be taken to mean that there is no place for state laws in the law of intellectual property. State unfair competition laws have coexisted with federal law in this area for quite some time, with little evidence of incompatibility. In the instant case, the Court indicated it had no inclination to strike down state trade secret or unfair competition laws.

WEIL CERAMICS AND GLASS, INC. v. DASH

878 F.2d 659, 11 U.S.P.Q.2d 1001 (3d Cir. 1989).

NATURE OF CASE: Appeal of summary judgment enjoining the importation and sale of foreign-made goods.

FACT SUMMARY: Weil ceramics (P), subsidiary of and exclusive agent for import of Lladro, S.A. statuary, sought to enjoin the import and sale of Lladro statuary.

CONCISE RULE OF LAW: A U.S. subsidiary/agent of a foreign manufacturer may not enjoin, under the Lanham Act and § 526 of the Tariff Act, the gray market importation of the manufacturer's goods.

FACTS: Weil Ceramics and Glass, Inc. (P) was purchased by Lladro, S.A., a Spanish corporation which manufactured ceramic statuary. Weil (P) was designated exclusive U.S. agent for the importation and sale of Lladro statuary. It came to Weil's (P) attention that Dash (D) was buying Lladro statuary in Spain and selling it in the United States. Weil (P) brought an action under the Lanham Act and § 526 of the Tariff Act, seeking to enjoin this practice. The district court entered summary judgment in favor of Weil (P) and enjoined Dash (D) from further importing the statuary. Dash (D) appealed.

ISSUE: May a U.S. subsidiary/agent of a foreign manufacturer enjoin, under the Lanham Act and § 526 of the Tariff Act, the gray market importation of the manufacturer's goods?

HOLDING AND DECISION: (Higginbotham, J.) No. A U.S. subsidiary/agent of a foreign manufacturer may not enjoin, under the Lanham Act and § 526 of the Tariff Act, the gray market importation of the manufacturer's goods. Section 526 prohibits importation of merchandise into the United States, if such merchandise bears a trademark and the U.S. bearer of that trademark does not authorize such importation. However, the U.S. Customs Agency, at 19 C.F.R. § 133.21, has interpreted this law to apply only where the U.S. trademark owner is a separate and independent entity from the foreign manufacturer. The Supreme Court has approved this interpretation, and it is conclusive here. As the Lanham Act, Weil (P) contends that the Act recognizes territoriality, and the owner of a trademark has the right to exclude all similar goods, even the same brand, from its territory. Again, the Supreme Court has only recognized this when the U.S. trademark owner is a separate entity that negotiated for trademark rights at arm's length. Such was not the case here. Finally, Weil (P) argued that § 42 of the Act prohibits the sale of goods that copy or simulate trademarked goods, and that unauthorized sales simulate a situation in which the goodwill of the products' maker is presented as backing the products, when in fact it is not. This is not the case. Trademark law does not reach the sale of genuine goods, even if the sale is unauthorized. For these reasons, neither the Tariff Act nor the Lanham Act prohibits the sale of the goods involved here. Reversed.

EDITOR'S ANALYSIS: The territoriality principle of which Weil (P) sought to avail itself was announced by the Supreme Court in A. Bourjois & Co. v. Katzel, 260 U.S. 689 (1923). This decision held that one purchasing goods from a foreign manufacturer could not sell them in the United States, when that manufacturer had conveyed an exclusive U.S. sales license. This ruling was predicated on the notion that the manufacturer should not benefit from sales in competition with its licensee. Where, as here, the licensee is controlled by the manufacturer, that rationale is inapplicable.

NOTES:

NOTES